## *"Prepare your heart to be moved!*

"Fire has the ability to warm, comfort, and give light. It can also burn stubble and purify gold. The fires of persecution purified the early Church and the Church in history. It still burns in many parts of this sinful world, and if God allows it to, it will blow our way. *Closer to the Fire: Lessons from the Persecuted Church* provides lessons we dare not ignore."

—**Ray Comfort,** Founder of Living Waters, TV co-host "The Way of the Master"

"*Closer to the Fire* is a factual reflection of the realities facing Christians around the world today. Not only did these compelling stories motivate me to pray for the persecuted church, but they also inspired some soul-searching. I wondered, 'What would I do if forced to defend my Christian faith under threat of death?'"

—**Gary Lane,** International News Director/Senior International Correspondent, CBN News

"Prepare your heart to be moved! Greg Musselman takes us to the front-lines to hear directly from believers who face persecution, imprisonment, and even death but stand strong for their faith. And the Church is growing because of this witness. He shows us how these believers challenge us to be more bold about our faith."

—**Janet Epp Buckingham,** Associate Professor at Trinity Western University, Director of the Laurentian Leadership Centre

"With the skill of a master storyteller Greg drew me into the harsh reality of the persecution that Christians face around the world. His style of writing, reflective of years in broadcasting, was concise and clear yet filled with the compassion that a Christian brother would have for those who suffer. Our students will learn much when they read this book."

—**Harold Rust**, President of the Canadian Lutheran Bible Institute, Camrose, Alberta

"In *Closer to the Fire* Greg Musselman brings us alongside into his experience as a Western Christian encountering the large body of the persecuted Church. Greg shares how God reached him personally with the reality of so much of the twenty-first century world's discrimination, imprisonment, beating, and murder of followers of Christ in country after country around the globe. He challenges the reader to hear the voices from the printed page, absorb the faces in the photographs, and respond to the suffering for Christ of our brothers and sisters. Don't keep this book to yourself. Please share it with your friends who may simply be unaware . . . and once aware they will find their life in Christ changed forever."

—**Don Hutchinson**, Vice President, The Evangelical Fellowship of Canada

"Thank you for sharing stories from our brothers and sisters around the world who are being persecuted. Their stories touch our heart and help us to remember the importance of forgiveness in our own lives, and how to be strategically praying for the persecuted Church and the ministries that work with them. Throughout the book you have challenged us in the West in so many ways in our own faith and to take up our cross, no matter the cost, to advance the kingdom."

—**Joan Hubert**, Executive Director, Missions Fest Alberta

# CLOSER *to the* FIRE

*Lessons from the*
*Persecuted Church*

## GREG MUSSELMAN
*with* TREVOR LUND

genesis
PUBLISHING GROUP

Closer to the Fire: Lessons from the Persecuted Church

Published by:
Genesis Publishing Group
2002 Skyline Place
Bartlesville, OK 74006
www.genesis-group.net

Edited by Lynn Copeland

Printed in the United States of America

ISBN 978-1-933591-11-7

*To persecuted Christians around the world:*
*our prayers and support are with you.*
*Your examples of courage and faith*
*encourage us more than you will*
*know on this side of heaven.*

# CONTENTS

# ACKNOWLEDGMENTS

First, I would like to thank my wife, Arlene, for her support and encouragement both to write this book and in my ministry with The Voice of the Martyrs. My being away from home on frequent travels puts an extra burden on her, and I am grateful for her patience. (Thanks so much, Arlene. I love you more than you can know!) My four children have also been great, and rarely complain when I am gone, whether traveling around the world or speaking in churches across Canada. They have been amazing!

I am grateful to Rev. Phillip Gagnon of St. Albert Evangelical Lutheran Church for his advice, friendship, and theological insight over many coffees, and to Trevor Lund, without whom this project might not have gotten off the ground. His creativity and desire to communicate kingdom stories through print was much needed and a blessing!

It was a privilege to have Lynn Copeland edit my book. Lynn is one of the best in the business! I appreciate my friends at The Voice of the Martyrs in Canada, as well as our VOM partners around the world who share a passion and love for the persecuted Church and who have contributed to my life in so many ways. And, of course, my heartfelt gratitude goes to our brothers and sisters in Christ who trusted me to tell their stories of suffering and victory. They not only allowed me to interview them, but in many cases we enjoyed wonderful times of fellowship and friendship because of our bond in Jesus.

Most importantly, and I do not want to trivialize this in any way, I want to thank my Lord Jesus Christ for entrusting me with the calling to serve His Church in this manner. It has been an amazing adventure!

# FOREWORD

I am honoured to have been asked to write this foreword for my good friend and brother in the Lord. It has been about five years since I have come to know Greg. Our talks together always encourage me as we have many interests in common and he never fails to impress me with his honest, down-to-earth manner. In those years I have come to appreciate his humour, friendship, and faith as a strong, vibrant brother in the Lord. Through those years I have also appreciated his ministry with The Voice of the Martyrs (VOM), a much-needed ministry that brings the stories of the persecuted Church to our awareness, especially to those in the West. The stories of Greg's life in VOM —and those whose lives touched his—will, in the following pages, no doubt touch yours.

Of course, reading these stories should touch our hearts. They are the stories of our brothers and sisters in the family of God who have suffered much on account of their faith, stories that intersect with ours. For as the ancient Irish prayer says, "Lord, be in us as we be in you, for if we be in you, we cannot be far from each other even if some be in heaven and some on earth." As such, we remember that we are bound together in Christ Jesus, rejoicing together, sorrowing together as we journey together whether separated by oceans and continents or this veil of tears. The separation of centuries or distance means nothing to the love and Spirit of Christ. But these stories are those of today, not those of the early Church and as such bring a sense of immediacy and wonder, bringing to mind the question, "Can these things truly be happening today?" Unfortunately, the answer is "Yes."

Greg's stories of his journey and those who have shared their struggles with him will challenge you to hear with your heart not only their sufferings, but especially their faith. The persecuted Church's stories should remind us that we are, indeed, not alone in our faith in the West and we have much to learn. In the last few years, I have come to share his concern and love for those whose families have experienced incredible tragedies and have been powerful witnesses to the unfailing presence and grace of our Lord in ways most would not expect. They have forgiven, stayed the course, and striven to follow Jesus wherever He would lead them. In many cases, they have even determined to become evangelists and pastors in order to bring the story of Jesus' love to those very same persecutors who sought their death.

Do not get me wrong, none of us are perfect and one would not want to romanticize the persecuted Church and discount their grief and humanity. But, thanks be to God, Jesus has not abandoned us to the world nor to ourselves. We are all sinners, beggars telling other beggars where to find bread at the table of the Lord and none are immune to feelings of anger, sorrow, and even vengeance. That being said, the persecuted Church teaches us to hear the gospel of grace in its fullness having been transformed by the Spirit through the crucible of suffering into the image of the Son. Who else can be so qualified to teach us, but those who have been refined through the fires of persecution and of the Spirit? Truly, when one is close to Jesus, one is close to the fire.

I know from our conversations that Greg has struggled with having seen and heard firsthand the stories of these brothers and sisters. One cannot experience, even second-hand, these stories without having your heart touched profoundly and then as Jesus calls us, weeping with those who weep. Sharing many a coffee with Greg, I share his conviction that many in the West have forgotten the meaning of suffering discipleship and dying to self. Dietrich Bonhoeffer, the Lutheran theologian who died in Flossenberg just before the end of WWII, wrote, "When Christ calls a man, He bids him come and die." Both of us reject the insipid theology of consumerism and cheap grace that plagues much of what is seen as cutting-edge and meaningful. We have placed the cart before the horse and have become distracted by things—possessions—rather than clinging to the God who gave us Himself. The truth is, the persecuted Church has so much to teach us about suffering, faithfulness, costly grace, and a love that is sacrificial and powerful in what appears to the world as weakness. The persecuted may appear to have little, but in Christ they have everything; whereas we, who appear to have everything, may, in fact, be found to have little. One has only to observe the trend of missionaries from various countries around the world coming to the West. Is it any wonder that the least would then speak to those who have so much? If only we would see and hear.

My hope and prayer is that you, the reader, will hear the hearts of those who have suffered, truly suffered for the sake of faithful discipleship to our Lord Jesus. I pray you will open your hearts and be renewed in your zeal and love: zeal for the Lord God who gave Himself for you; love for your neighbour, across the street and across the ocean, for whom Jesus died. I thank God for those like Greg who travel the world over, entering not-so-friendly places and then returning to tell us the stories trying to shake us up. They call us to remember to Whom we belong. They also remind us who we are, today, this moment, in Christ Jesus—together as one Body, with one Spirit, one Lord, one faith, one baptism, and one God and Father (Ephesians 4:4–6). In a way, I believe that God inhabits these stories, as they are ultimately stories of His faithfulness, His love working through jars of clay, and His truth shining brightly in refined hearts and minds. All that we are is from Him.

In closing, I am reminded of the saying, "We ought to pray like it all depends on God and work like it all depends on us." May God continue to bless Greg, the ministry of The Voice of the Martyrs, and especially the martyrs and their families. May God strengthen us in what we are doing to serve and remember the persecuted Church, forgive us for not doing what is within us to do, and bring us into the fullness of His Son. May it be so among us.

REV. PHILLIP GAGNON STS
St. Albert Evangelical Lutheran Church
St. Albert, Alberta

# PREFACE

In the dozen years I have been working with The Voice of the Martyrs Canada, I have interviewed countless Christians around the world who have suffered hardship and persecution for their decision to follow Christ or be identified with Him. Their stories are often tragic, but always moving, and frequently reveal a deeper hope and a greater faith than I could ever experience in my own protected walk. It has been humbling to meet with them and see their faith, and it is a privilege to share their stories.

We all go through difficulties in life and some of us endure tragic events, although for Christians in the West these difficulties are not usually a direct result of our faith. Like the individuals you will read about in these pages, the choices we make determine our outlook and depth of spiritual maturity. Because these believers chose to rely on the Lord and the truths of Scripture, they were able to overcome even in the midst of tremendous adversity. It is my hope that their examples will help you examine your own choices in the circumstances you face.

That is what has happened to me as I have interviewed my brothers and sisters about the persecution they have endured. Do not think the truths from their stories do not apply to you. The circumstances of their persecution may seem unreal, but the decisions they faced are the same ones many of us have as we encounter difficulties in life.

Each chapter will include a verse and at times my understanding of that verse from a safe, North American perspective. Then the stories I share will reinforce the truth of that Scripture or perhaps shatter the misconceptions I had about its interpretation. Finally, we will take a look at its deeper significance, and you will be challenged to ask yourself some probing questions to help you strengthen your own personal walk.

Thank you for coming on this journey with me to learn from our persecuted brothers and sisters who are willing to suffer for their Saviour. It is my prayer that the stories in this book will empower you to experience a greater trust in God and to make the choice to walk closer to the fire.

# CHAPTER 1

# NO RETREAT

*"And from the days of John the Baptist until now the kingdom of heaven suffers violence, and the violent take it by force."*
MATTHEW 11:12

On January 5, around forty members of the Deeper Life Bible Church in northeastern Nigeria were gathered for an evening prayer meeting in their modest, one-room church building. Pastor Chenma Ngwaba was leading the committed group of believers, from small children to the elderly. As he was standing at the pulpit guiding the group in prayer, he suddenly heard gunshots. He looked up to see three armed attackers outside, shooting into the church. "As they started firing," Chenma said, "I saw people through the windows shooting everybody there."

They were under attack by the militant Muslim group Boko Haram, whose aim is to rid much of the country of Christians.

Chenma quickly dove behind the pulpit to avoid being shot. "I had to crawl on the floor and try to get outside," the pastor said, "and as I crawled I realized that I had been shot in the stomach." As he made his way through the chaos inside the church, he saw many of his church members lying on the ground wounded—or dead. "I saw my wife, with our eighteen-month-old baby in her arms. My wife was already dead, but the baby was not hurt."

This senseless attack by the three young men with Boko Haram lasted just a few minutes and claimed the lives of ten people that night. Chenma lost not only his beloved thirty-six-year-old wife, Silfa, but also his ten-year-old son, Jeremiah. Two dozen other believers had been injured.

For more than a decade, I have been conducting hundreds of interviews with persecuted Christians from around the globe bringing their stories to believers in the free world, including my home country of Canada. As I traveled to Nigeria in early 2012 to meet with Christians who were suffering for the gospel, I talked with surviving members of the Deeper Life Bible Church in Gombe's Bogo District. Chenma's story was one of many we gathered during our three-day stay in Gombe. The tragic stories that he and other believers shared with us sparked feelings of grief, sorrow, and outrage. Yet we were also amazed at the faith of these Christians after such a vicious attack.

From a biblical point of view I understand why Christians are oppressed, jailed, tortured, and even killed for their faith in Jesus Christ. Christian persecution has been occurring for two thousand years and will continue until the Lord's return. Even though there is a strong scriptural basis to explain why these horrible events happen, the brutality against our brothers and sisters in Christ is still hard to comprehend.

I was first introduced to the reality of Christian persecution through Brother Andrew's ministry, Open Doors. At that time, something significant gripped my heart. Although I had been a Christian for six years, I had never heard about the persecuted Church. I thought that persecution was all in the past—something that happened to the Early Church in the Roman Coliseum. Hearing the stories of Christians who were suffering today because of their faith in Jesus Christ and discovering the horrible things that had been done to them touched me deeply and I felt compelled to do something. Since then, as my awareness of the subject has grown, my passion to help these believers has intensified.

As I have struggled to comprehend the blatant brutality against God's people, the words of Jesus have given me hope. He said, "And from the days of John the Baptist until now the kingdom of heaven suffers violence, and the violent take it by force" (Matthew 11:12). What is clear from this verse, and many others, is that the Church is involved in a battle. Though it is primarily a battle in the spiritual realm, its effects are also visible in the physical world.

The physical casualties in this war between God's kingdom and the kingdom of darkness are staggering. Even in the twenty-first century, tens of thousands of Christians are killed every year. It is impossible to know with certainty the exact number of believers martyred for their faith annually. However, according to the World Evangelical Alliance, each year more than 200 million followers of Christ in at least sixty countries are denied fundamental human rights solely because of their faith.

There are many examples in countries around the world where one can see the intensity and viciousness of this attack against Christians. I would like to introduce you to several of these believers—your brothers and sisters in Christ—who have faced such brutality, yet they embrace the hope that Jesus is the ultimate Victor in the battle. As you meet them, you will be encouraged by their refusal to retreat in the face of violence. Allow their testimonies of courage to inspire you to stand strong in the midst of your own battles.

## The Church Under Attack in Orissa, India

One of the nations where Christians face persecution is India, specifically the state of Orissa (official spelling was recently changed to Odisha). In Orissa, followers of Jesus are very aware of this spiritual war. They have witnessed firsthand the anger of those who hate the gospel, yet they refuse to retreat.

On January 22, 1999, the murders of Australian missionary Graham Staines and his two young sons, Philip and Timothy, brought worldwide attention to the difficulties Christians faced in Orissa from militant Hindu groups attempting to destroy Christianity. Though Hinduism is traditionally considered peaceful and tolerant toward other beliefs, a militant movement within the religion was aiming to rid India of all other faiths. The rise of Hindutva ("India is Hindu only") extremism resulted in hate campaigns against Muslims in the early 1990s and against Christians in the late 1990s, as followers of "foreign" religions. By 1999, this movement had indisputably resorted to violence.

*The Staines family*

Graham brought his medical skills to Orissa to help lepers, but he and his wife, Gladys, a nurse, also brought the love of Christ. As they faithfully served the people of the area for three decades, bringing them help and hope, Hindu extremists took notice of the conversions and decided that the Staines family must be stopped. While away from home during a five-night evangelistic outreach, Graham and his two sons, ages nine and seven, were surrounded by a mob and burned alive in their station wagon as they slept. Villagers seeing the attack were prevented from rescuing them. Since then, widespread attacks against Christians in Orissa have escalated. Believers have been killed or badly injured, and their homes, shops, and churches have been burned.

In December 2007 and August 2008, unprecedented mob violence against Christians erupted in Orissa. The August attacks followed the assassination of World Hindu Council leader Swami Laxmanananda Saraswati. Although Maoist (communist) guerrillas claimed responsibility for the leader's murder, Hindu militants used it as an excuse to attack Christians throughout the state—leaving over one hundred dead, tens of thousands displaced, and hundreds of church buildings and thousands of Christians' homes destroyed. India's constitution guarantees freedom of religion and at times arrests those

*Destruction in Orissa*

responsible, but local authorities often turn a blind eye or are afraid to take action. With religious violence of this magnitude, there seemed to be little they could do to protect the Christians once the mob attacks began.

Though the level of violence was new, the persecution of Christians in Orissa was not. Reverend Sudhakar Mondithoka of the Hyderabad Institute of Theology and Apologetics stated that this had been happening for decades. He considered it "quite natural that the worst persecution in the entire history of our country should have been witnessed in that state." He went on to explain that Christianity "has grown significantly in some of those blocks, within that Kandhamal District. There is one place where Christians are 90 per cent, and so the extreme fundamentalist Hindu people have been waiting for an opportunity to do something that will put an end to this growth of Christianity."

Over four hundred church buildings in the Kandhamal District were destroyed in the August 2008 attacks, including the Baptist church in Damba where Joseph Nayak was the pastor. He and his family were fortunate to escape after the radical Hindu mob came to their village intent on attacking it. "When the Christians in the village saw houses and church buildings on fire, they ran from the village," said Pastor Joseph. "The people were completely unprepared and left with only the clothes on their backs." He and his fellow villagers fled to a nearby hill and waited, helpless as their homes were attacked.

When the villagers returned in the evening, their church building was in ruins. "When we saw it broken up, it hurt us," said Pastor Joseph. "In this church we not only worshiped on Sundays, but on other days we conducted youth programs, prayer fellowships, and events for men, women, and children."

Pastor Joseph of course knows that the Church is the people, not the building, but still, he said, "It was so hard, because

we worshiped Jesus in this building." The violence did not cause his congregation to stop their ministry, however, and they are now even more fully aware of the battle against the kingdom of darkness.

*Pastor Joseph inside his church*

As in any war, this battle has resulted in casualties. There are countless victims and survivors in this assault on the Body of Christ, and I had the privilege of meeting several when I traveled with a VOM team to Orissa in 2009. In the midst of their pain and hardship, these believers were standing strong, setting an example of unwavering faith in the Lord Jesus. One of them is a woman named Puspanjali Panda.

## Puspanjali Panda: "My Husband Is with the Lord"

Puspanjali's life dramatically changed after the violent events that swept through her village. Her husband, Dibya, was the pastor of the Baptist church in Raykia, located in the Kandhamal District. His death left Puspanjali a widow and their ten-year-old daughter, Mona Lisha, without a father.

On Sunday, August 23, 2008, Dibya told Puspanjali to head home with their daughter after the church service and he would join them after he finished some business at the church. While working, he heard loud noises outside and saw that a Hindu mob had surrounded the village. This was not the first time these Hindu extremists had come to the village to attack the Christians. They had been active the previous two months and had threatened to kill them. Concerned for his safety as well as his family's, Dibya sought refuge at a friend's house.

*Puspanjali Panda*

Two days later, a mob of two hundred men showed up and dragged him from his friend's house, severely beating him. They knew he was a pastor and that he was reaching many Hindus with his preaching. With tears running down her face, Puspanjali told me that the hate-filled mob showed no mercy to the man she loved and admired. "When the mob drove him out of the house, they accused him of preaching Christ and 'making Christians.' They threw rocks at his head and punched him in the face, yelling, 'You preach with this mouth!'"

As blood was streaming out of his mouth, Dibya asked his attackers if he could see his wife and daughter and say his last words to them. They told him, "No, no, we won't let you because you are converting people and making them change their religion." They continued beating him until he was unconscious, then they put a large rock around his neck and threw him into the river.

Two days passed before Puspanjali discovered that her husband had been murdered. As she and her daughter waited to learn of his whereabouts, Mona Lisha insisted on looking for him. They eventually came across his lifeless body, which had been recovered from the river. "My daughter saw that her father was dead, and she started to cry," Puspanjali said. Puspanjali told her grieving daughter, "God knows everything about what happened and why it happened. He will take care of us." Despite her distress and heartbreak, Mona Lisha replied, "If they want to kill us like they killed Papa, don't worry, Mama, we'll also stand for Him."

*"If they want to kill us like they killed Papa, don't worry, Mama, we'll also stand for Him."*

Puspanjali believed her husband was targeted by the Hindu mob because of his work in the village. "When my husband started the work there, only eight families were Christians," she said. "When people were sick, he would pray for them, and miracles would take place. Just a couple months later, twenty-eight families had come to the Lord, and that is the reason he was killed."

After the murder of her husband, Puspanjali—a former Hindu—went to live with her parents in a predominantly Hindu village. She was warned by the Hindu extremists that she would also be murdered if she stayed. At that time, her daughter was living in a Christian hostel in another part of the state for her safety.

Puspanjali said she wanted to stay and be a witness among the people in the village, adding, "I'm also praying that those who killed my husband will come to faith in Christ. Sometimes it's hard to forgive, but when I get back to the Word of God it gives me inspiration to forgive them."

## Purna Digal:
## "I Didn't Think I Would Survive"

Purna Chandra Digal, a husband and father of eight, bears the scars of the August 2008 riots that nearly claimed his life. Purna said he knew he and his family were in trouble when he heard the loud commotion of an angry mob entering the village. "At 11:00 in the evening, they were shouting slogans to their Hindu gods. There were about a hundred and fifty peo-

ple," Purna recalled. He quickly took his family to the jungle where they could hide, then he came back to the village and watched help- lessly as the mob set his house on fire. When he thought it was safe, Purna re- turned to their bad-

*Purna Digal*

ly burned home to gather some of the family's remaining belongings—a decision that almost cost him his life. "The mob returned and attacked me," Purna said. "They beat me brutally with big sticks and slashed my face with a knife." He was beaten so badly on the legs that it crippled him.

During the attack, Purna told us, he could do nothing but pray for help. "I said to the Lord that many people have come prepared with swords and sticks. 'Lord, I can't do anything. I am all alone, and You are my only fortress, so take care of me.' I was bleeding severely and didn't think I would survive." Purna then lost consciousness, and the mob left him to die. Soon after, two Christians from his village found him and took him to a hospital in a neighbouring village where he received basic first aid. "When my wife heard about what happened to me, she and one of my daughters came and took me back to the jungle," Purna said. The family remained in hiding until the violence ended.

After Purna, his wife, Basanti, and their children had spent three days in the jungle, they were found by a group of fifteen Hindu militants who were pursuing those who had fled. "We were threatened that if we didn't go back to our village and stay there, they would take our lives," he explained. "That night we returned to our village."

Four days after the brutal attack, Purna finally received proper medical care. Later, his family went to live in a nearby relief camp set up by the government. It was just too dangerous for the Christians to remain in the village. When I talked with Purna, he still appeared to be in pain and said he was not doing well physically. "For three months, I was unable to get up from my bed. I got treatment at a Christian medical place."

Despite their losses, Purna was thankful to the Lord that he and his family were still alive. "No one in my village died, but in a nearby village, four or five people I knew had died."

Purna believed he was targeted because it was well known that he was a Christian active in sharing the gospel with Hindus. The attack that left him injured and his family's home destroyed has not weakened his faith; in fact, it has had the opposite effect. "Through this I know that God has helped me, so that increased my faith. There are three hundred families in the area where I now live, and we are the only Christian family," Purna added. "I want to see my children grow in their faith and see them in the mission field so through my children these three hundred families may come to the Lord."

## Saphira: "He Prayed for Them"

Saphira Nayak's story is not uncommon for believers living under persecution in several of India's states and in other countries around the world. Saphira has suffered the loss of loved ones due to attacks against their faith. In late August 2008, her father and grandmother's lives came to a violent end when a mob of a hundreds of Hindu extremists showed up in her Christian village. The mob's goal was to cause as much destruction as possible to the Christians living there. "Two to three hundred of the people who came had different kinds of weapons," Saphira recalled of that frightening day. "Many had their faces covered with masks. They broke into all the houses and set all our belongings on fire."

Saphira's father, fifty-five-year-old Samuel, was confronted by the angry mob.

*Saphira Nayak*

Saphira remembered how her father, a pastor for thirty years, stood firm and even prayed for them. "They came to my father and told him to deny Jesus, but he refused. When he refused to deny Jesus, they laughed, mocking him," Saphira explained. "He told them, 'You can do whatever you want to my body; it's not my body and I won't deny Jesus.' He then asked them if he could pray for a few minutes. He prayed for them so they might receive forgiveness."

Saphira, very emotional and at times struggling to speak as she relived this horrible event, said that while her father was praying, the mob beat and stabbed him, then after lighting a fire they threw him into the flames. "They brought kerosene along with them, and they put my father in the fire," she told me. He died soon afterwards. Saphira's grandmother was also killed during the rampage, and her body was also burned. Saphira, her husband, and their four children, ages six to twelve, were able to escape. After three days, the mob took her father's remains and threw them into a river near Saphira's village.

Though she misses her father, Saphira is grateful for his courage as he stood strong for Jesus even until death. "We are proud of him, but we sometimes feel lonely," Saphira said, adding that she will always remember something her father said to the people of his church before he was martyred. "I might die, and even after my death you might be persecuted," he told his congregation. "So when they come to persecute you and physically torture you, never deny Jesus. Stand on the faith."

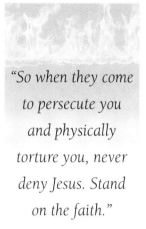

*"So when they come to persecute you and physically torture you, never deny Jesus. Stand on the faith."*

Saphira still faces many challenges. For one, her husband does not have a strong Christian faith, as she has. "He is trying to get me to deny Jesus. Pray that my husband will be one with me. God is in control of everything, so that gives me courage to go on."

Saphira said she has just one desire: "My father brought us up in the faith. I want to bring my children up the same way, to be stronger and stronger in the faith." Like her father, Saphira knows that proclaiming the gospel and leading people into God's kingdom do not go unnoticed by enemies of the gospel.

As the Staines family, Pastor Joseph Nayak, Puspanjali, Purna, and Saphira have discovered firsthand, suffering is a normal part of proclaiming the gospel. After all, the One they follow has told them, "If the world hates you, you know that it hated Me before it hated you...Remember the word that I said to you, 'A servant is not greater than his master.' If they persecuted Me, they will also persecute you" (John 15:18–20).

## OUR CHALLENGE:
## ENGAGE VERSUS RETREAT

So much of what is taught in North American churches implies that when we suffer, it is because we did something wrong, not because we did something right. But in nations where religious freedoms are restricted, I often meet Christians who, when persecuted, follow the example of the apostles after they were beaten by religious leaders: "So they departed from the presence of the council, rejoicing that they were counted worthy to suffer shame for His name. And daily in the temple, and in every house, they did not cease teaching and preaching Jesus as the Christ" (Acts 5:41,42). They refused to retreat. Instead, they *rejoiced*.

Scripture lays it out very clearly: suffering for Christ is normal and even expected. In the Beatitudes, Jesus told His disciples, "Blessed are you when men hate you, and when they exclude you, and revile you, and cast out your name as evil, for the Son of Man's sake. Rejoice in that day and leap for joy! For indeed your reward is great in heaven, for in like manner their fathers did to the prophets" (Luke 6:22,23). Notice again that suffering is not only normal, but is cause for *rejoicing*.

Have you experienced rejection from family or friends as you have shared Christ with them? On some level, all of us who want others to know about God's love for them will experience ridicule and rejection. Hopefully it is not as dramatic as the incidents you have read about in this chapter, but likely you have had some experience with being rejected because of your faith. Too many of us let that fear of rejection keep us from telling others about God's forgiveness and grace. We excuse ourselves from being active in sharing the gospel because we do not want to be offensive to others.

However, Paul wrote to Philemon, "I pray that you may be active in sharing your faith, so that you will have a full understanding of every good thing we have in Christ" (Philemon 1:6,

NIV1984). We cannot have a full understanding of every good thing we have in Christ if we are not active in sharing our faith.

There is a very simple, inoffensive way to start being active in sharing your faith: begin by sharing other people's faith. Tell others the stories you have read in this chapter. Talk about the incredible faith seen in the face of overwhelming tragedy. Through this sharing, you will start to have a fuller understanding of the good things you have in Christ.

 CONSIDER & SHARE

- Without complaining, can you tell someone about an experience you have had with personal suffering?

- Think about a time when you knew you should talk with someone about Christ, but fear made you stop. Are you more or less likely to share today? Explain. Does realizing that God is loving and patient with you make you more or less likely to share?

- When was the last time you told someone about the good things God has done for you? Ask God to help you to share about it today, and then choose to take advantage of the opportunity He brings.

# CHAPTER 2

# ADVANCING THE KINGDOM

*"On this rock I will build My church, and the
gates of Hades shall not prevail against it."*
MATTHEW 16:18

I have often thought that this verse in Matthew described the Church in a defensive posture because it was always under attack. I thought Jesus was telling His disciples, both then and throughout history, that no matter how bad the situation became for them, there would be a Church standing when He returned. I envisioned the Church as a fortified city under siege with constant bombardment from enemy troops. While believers around the world, including those of us in the "free world," may at times feel like we are barely holding down the fort, that is not the situation portrayed in the New Testament.

True, the Church is in a battle against the kingdom of darkness—from both within and without. To understand this, keep in mind that the Church is not a building, but the people who have been redeemed by the blood of Christ. The Church is the Body of Christ (1 Corinthians 12:27). This relationship with Jesus puts us into a family where we have brothers and sisters all over the world!

While there will continue to be martyrs for Jesus until the end of time (Revelation 6:9–11), we know that our Lord has won the war between His kingdom and the kingdom of darkness. Believers are not locked in a barricaded building hoping to avoid capture; instead, we are marching on the enemy's turf. Rather than protecting us from the enemy, the "gates of Hades" actually protect the domain of Satan. Think about it.

What did gates do in ancient times? They let people in and out of a city and were usually closed when the city was under attack. When Jesus said, "The gates of Hades shall not prevail against [the church]," His intent was that the Church would be advancing against the kingdom of Satan.

The main reason for all the casualties in this war is that the gospel is moving forward. Even in the most repressive regimes in the world, people are coming to know Jesus as their Lord and Saviour. No matter how hard dictators and their regimes, militant religious leaders and their followers try to wipe out the Church, it will not happen. Many have tried, but in the end, Jesus will be victorious.

North Korea is an example of a nation where following Christ can mean imprisonment, torture, and even death. However, there are those who are committed to seeing the gospel come into the lives of the oppressed people of North Korea. One such person is Mr. Kim,[1] a man who is determined to bring the message of God's love through Jesus Christ to his former homeland.

## Mr. Kim: Bringing Jesus to the "Evil Empire"

Despite three government-run churches in Pyongyang, the capital city, it is illegal to be a Christian in North Korea. These churches, the only ones allowed by the government, are strictly controlled by the regime and are primarily for appearances. True believers must worship secretly in underground churches. Most Christian organizations like The Voice of the Martyrs consider the nation of North Korea to be one of the most, if not the most, dangerous in the world to be a follower of Christ.

---

1 His full name is not used for security reasons.

Hundreds of thousands of Christians have died because of persecution, and up to 35,000 are currently in prisons or work camps. The true number of Christians is unknown, though estimated by most reliable sources to be around 100,000.

*Kim*

Mr. Kim escaped the clutches of North Korea in the mid-1990s, and shares his story of the plight of people living in his former homeland with anyone who will listen, including world leaders. Kim fled the country after becoming disillusioned by its horrible conditions and nearly constant bouts of famine. Due to economic mismanagement and poor allocation of resources, chronic food shortages and widespread malnutrition have been rampant for decades. When Kim spoke of the brutal conditions there, he said, "Every day I heard the news of executions from more than twenty political concentration camps all over North Korea and news of three million people who starved or froze to death."

As a captain in the military, Kim would face severe penalties for his decision to desert the military and leave North Korea. He escaped to China, where he met some Christians who shared the gospel with him, and he even participated in singing worship songs to God. Still, it was only when Chinese authorities caught him and sent him back to North Korea that Kim put his trust in Jesus Christ. (China has an agreement with North Korea to return those who have fled the country.)

"When I was sent from China back to North Korea there was a bridge. As I crossed the bridge I knew I was going to die," Kim told me. "I knew this was my time of destiny. I wanted to sing a praise song to the Lord, but I couldn't remember any I had heard, so I promised myself that if I lived and escaped again I would learn praise songs and memorize them."

While Kim had served in the North Korean military, he had written poems and songs about the greatness of the former leader of North Korea, Kim Il Sung. One of Kim's works even became required memorization for the country's soldiers. Since becoming a Christian, he has written songs praising the God of heaven.

Considered a traitor for abandoning the military and fleeing the country, Kim was brutally beaten and had his fingers broken. After being sentenced to death in Onsung, North Korea, some of the men Kim had served with determined that he should be sent by train to Pyongyang, where he would be executed for treason. Facing certain death, Kim knew that unless he did something drastic his life on earth would soon be over. So he took action. "On the third day I felt the presence of the soldiers who were guarding me behind me. I could tell one of them was hesitating before going through a door," he explained. "I knew this was my only chance to escape. Without thinking I jumped off the moving train by leaping through the window. My body aged a thousand years at that moment."

Incredibly, Kim survived the jump from the moving train. Despite being badly bruised and suffering some broken bones, he made his way back into China and reconnected with the Christians he had met there before. Kim spent the next two and a half years working in a charcoal factory, growing in his relationship with Jesus and copying the entire Bible before going to South Korea in 1999. When we met, Kim was active in trying to reach North Koreans with the message of God's love through a daily half-hour, shortwave radio broadcast that focused on Christian persecution. He believed that the only hope for the land of his birth was Jesus Christ. "North Korea is an empire of evil. The world has nothing to do with them," he told me. "They don't have a principle of law; they shoot missiles, sell drugs, and make counterfeit dollars. The only way forward is to melt the North Korean hearts with love and the gospel."

Despite what seem like insurmountable obstacles, the Church is advancing in North Korea. No matter how hard the country's leaders try to stop the Word of God, people like Kim are still faithful to God's calling. Later in this book, you will meet other North Korean Christians who are desperately trying to bring the light of the gospel into the darkness of this Hermit Kingdom.

## The Return of the Church in Northern Pakistan

Another country where the Church faces intense opposition, hardship, and persecution is the Islamic Republic of Pakistan. However, because of a great love for God and His kingdom, the followers of Jesus are advancing instead of retreating.

Northern Pakistan contains rugged mountains featuring some of the highest peaks in the world, helping to attract visitors from all over the globe. The region became a part of Pakistan in 1948—a year after the country gained independence from British India. Pakistan is bordered by Afghanistan, China, and India, with over ninety-nine per cent of the 1.7 million people in the Northern Area considering themselves Muslims. Although less than one per cent identify themselves as Christians today, Christianity once thrived in this part of the country. In the fourteenth century the ruler converted to Islam and massacred the Christian population, erasing all non-Muslim expressions of religion and destroying all the churches in the region.

A prominent Pakistani Christian leader told me that persecution is "a part of the church history in that area where so many people were assassinated. But a lot of historians do not know this part of the church history, so it's very important that the Church comes to know what happened there." For the most part, the history of Christianity in northern Pakistan has been erased from the history books.

Pastor "Parvez"[2] in northern Pakistan added, "There were so many Christians living here centuries ago and the blood of the Christian martyrs is in this land. God does not forget the blood of the martyrs. Whatever we are doing here I believe is the answer to their prayers, and God who is on the throne remembers."

For over six hundred years, this entire region—which covers over 72,000 kilometres—was without a church building. That drought came to an end in 2006 when an evangelical church officially opened and a dream was realized.

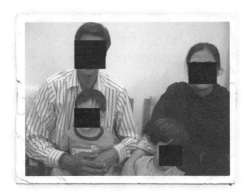

*Pastor "Parvez" and his family*

Parvez came to northern Pakistan in 2000 after graduating from Bible school. He said that he was clearly directed to come to the area. "While I was in Bible college," Parvez stated, "the Lord called me to the northern area of Pakistan. I had a dream in which I saw myself standing beside the river. There were many people wearing hats from the northern area, and they were calling my name, 'Please come to our area.' I saw many people coming to Jesus Christ and I understood that God was calling me to serve Him in this place."

Parvez said the strategy for building the Church in this area was simple and straightforward. Go to those who identified themselves as Christians, even if they were Christian in name only, and disciple them. Before long, these people were transformed into passionate followers of Jesus Christ. In the years that followed, the fellowship has grown in maturity and in

2 When a pseudonym is used to protect an individual's identity, the first occurrence is shown in quotation marks.

numbers, and with the help of The Voice of the Martyrs Canada, a church building was constructed in 2006.

Pastor Parvez is married and has two young children. He said his wife, "Rachel," is also called to this work, which at times is very difficult and dangerous. In spite of the risks, Rachel is completely committed to the ministry. "I personally believe, and my family believes,

*The first recent church building in northern Pakistan*

we are called by the Lord," she told me. "We are in the will of God. We are a part of God's plan. As long as it is His will that we serve, we believe that no one can touch us. But if it is His will that we shed our blood as martyrs, we consider it a joy and we are not afraid."

Every morning Rachel prays for her family. "I ask the Lord for the protection that is in the blood of Jesus. I pray for myself, I pray for my husband, I pray for the church compound, the church, the house," she explained. "I know that the blood of Jesus is stronger than any evil force. This praying time gives me great comfort, joy, and a sense of security."

Before meeting her husband, Rachel was intensely praying, "Lord, reveal Your will, 100 per cent upon me. I want to marry a person who is called to do Your will. I don't want less than that." And God answered her prayers. She said of Parvez, "God showed me very clearly that this was the man I was to marry."

Rachel has needed the assurance of her call to this ministry as it has been very difficult and unsettling at times, such as when she received a greatly disturbing phone call. "It was very threatening. Very dirty language was spoken to me. They threatened to kill me, kidnap me," she recalled, "They also said they would harm my husband and children and kill them. This was very shocking for me as a woman. I did feel pressure, but again God's peace came and my fears were gone, and I'm encouraged to serve God knowing that He has sent me here."

Parvez and Rachel envision more than just one church and ministry centre for the northern region. They want to further advance God's kingdom. "When the church was founded, I had to communicate the vision to the members," Parvez stated. "Now I'm sure that the church also has the same vision that I do, and that the Lord is using us all."

Parvez and his team had no transportation when they started going to other villages throughout the region, so they would walk seven to ten hours a day. "We were doing the evangelism work on foot for almost two years. Then we got motorbikes, and for the next year and a half we were on motorbikes," said Parvez. A jeep was eventually given to the pastor and his team, enabling them to access more villages and give out over 30,000 Christian books. "We came many times. We were caught by the police in the districts. We were followed by Muslims. We were threatened. We were warned by the authorities," Parvez told me. "But still God keeps bringing us to this region. He has a plan and purpose for this district."

Rachel heads up the Women's Vocational Centre, which both Christians and Muslims attend. One of the goals of the centre is to help women in the community to be able to support themselves and their families by developing skills and starting their own businesses. Many obstacles had to be overcome to bring these women of different religions and sects together. For centuries Sunni and Shia Muslims have been separated by mistrust and hatred. When it comes to being with Christian women, that is something Muslim females just do not do. They are taught that Christians are immoral. It would also be unthinkable for these Muslim women to come to a church building.

Rachel said many of these women had difficulties getting their family's permission to come. "Some are from a very socially restricted area [dominated by the Taliban] and were not free to leave their homes. Sometimes their parents or uncles stopped them from coming. They had to struggle to convince them that it was useful for them. Yet after crossing all these hurdles, they ended up in the sewing centre."

Rachel has seen how friendships and trust have developed between the Christian and Muslim women, in addition to the training. "Every day we start our classes with a word of prayer. Then we give health lessons from a Christian point of view," she explained, which cover basic hygiene, caring for their bodies, and treating them with respect. "Also, through our attitudes and our conversations, they see the love of God that comes from our hearts to them."

As a result, many of these Muslims become curious about Christianity and ask questions. Some have even come to Sunday services and have asked for Bibles and Christian books. "Before the opening of the sewing centre, the general view held by the Muslims was that Christians were not good people because they give so much freedom to their women," said Rachel. "But when their women come here for a year, they see we are good and moral people, so that concept has been changed in their minds."

A twenty-nine-year-old mother of three told me how she has faced many challenges trying to support her family, especially being a Christian in a Muslim-dominated area. "The sewing centre has helped so much. Before, we felt dependent on other people for clothes for my children and for me. Now, with the sewing centre training, I no longer feel dependent on other people. This has been a great help and blessing for the women of the area," she said.

The Women's Vocational Centre was so successful that a second floor was added to the church building, again with help from Christians in other parts of the world. The believers in the area are very grateful, and one said, "We Christians are all one, and we are concerned about each other."

Both women and men are also trained for ministry by Parvez, who teaches them to share the gospel throughout the region and plant churches, many of which are "underground" churches due to the presence of militant groups like the Taliban. One of the young evangelists mentored by Pastor Parvez is Haroon. Haroon is from a military background and has been a Christian for only a few years, but he has a deep desire to spread the gospel and see many come to Jesus. His ministry has not been without difficulties and danger. "When I share Jesus with my Muslim friends, I receive a lot of threats that I would be kicked out of my job, or I would be killed. This was so much stress and pressure on me. I was crying and discouraged."

Haroon went to his pastor and told him what was happening. The pastor encouraged him to stand strong in his faith. Haroon said that he took those words to heart, and that has made all the difference. "I had the fire of God's love in my heart," he said. "That fire motivated me to go and share Jesus Christ."

When we met with Haroon, he was working in an area that is almost 100 per cent Muslim. He knew the risks and dangers, but this young husband and father of two small children was willing to do whatever the Lord asked of him. "Yes, because Jesus Himself died for me. I have made a commitment to Him that I will serve Him even if I have to go through hardships," he declared. "Wherever He sends me I'm willing to go, even to the hardest places on the earth."

Jesus promised that the gates of Hades would not prevail against His Church, but for over six centuries that promise did not seem to be a reality in northern Pakistan. The church in that area had been all but destroyed until some young men and women got a vision to go there, in spite of danger and resistance, and once again build Christ's Church.

## OUR CHALLENGE:
## ADVANCING AS ONE BODY

Working against what appeared to be incredible odds, intense opposition, and a bloodied church in countries like North Korea and Pakistan, God's work not only survived but moved forward and grew in numbers of disciples.

In sports, it is often said that "a good defence leads to a good offence." This means that if you look after your own end of the field, it will lead to opportunities on the other team's end. That is not how it works when it comes to God's kingdom, as true victory comes from moving forward and advancing. If Kim and our friends in Pakistan did not push forward by bringing people to Christ, there would be very little to defend. There are many Scriptures that deal with battle, and one of the most important recognizes that the battle we are fighting is not on the human level.

The apostle Paul stated very clearly to the believers in Ephesus that the war we are fighting is a spiritual one: "For we do not wrestle against flesh and blood, but against principalities, against powers, against the rulers of the darkness of this age, against spiritual hosts of wickedness in the heavenly places" (Ephesians 6:12). Yet Paul also knew the physical toll that following Christ took on his life (2 Corinthians 11:23–27). While the battle was won at the cross, the struggle will never leave us this side of heaven.

Kim, Parvez, and the others understand that very well. As believers expand the reach of the message of the cross, dark spiritual forces fight back. We do not need to be afraid of them. What is true for the Church in every part of the world is true in our personal relationship with Christ in the free world.

Just as Jesus builds the Church, so will the Father finish the work that He has started in us as individuals. Paul promises us that "He who has begun a good work in you will complete it until the day of Jesus Christ" (Philippians 1:6). Christ is building His Church and the gates of Hades will not prevail against it. We can trust that God can and will accomplish both—He will build His Church and finish His work in us as individuals.

I know when you hear stories such as these you may be thinking, *How would I handle that kind of persecution?* If you have not experienced much heartache in life, you may think you would easily give everything for Christ. All of us should be thankful for God's grace on our lives and work to extend that grace to others. But if we seriously wonder how we would stand up under persecution, we should never forget that God is faithful. Even if we face persecution, God is committed to completing the work He wants us to do here.

## CONSIDER & SHARE

- If you were faced with the same trials you have read about in these pages, how do you honestly think you would respond? What makes you certain that is what you would do?

- If you are afraid to share your faith because someone may be offended, do you think you would refuse to deny Jesus when your life was threatened? Explain why or why not.

- Haroon was willing to serve Jesus through any hardships and go even to "the hardest places on earth." Where is a "hard place" in your area that you can go to this week to help advance God's kingdom? Think of a place where you can share with someone about God, then go do it.

# CHAPTER 3

# THEY KNOW NOT WHAT THEY DO

*"Jesus said, 'Father, forgive them,*
*for they do not know what they do.'"*
LUKE 23:34

I was on staff in a church and, during the first year of the ministry, things went really well. There was a strong emphasis on evangelism. People were coming to Christ out of some pretty tough backgrounds, and many were reengaging with church after being gone for a number of years. Things were going great. The second year, the pastor was determined to go in a certain direction, and anyone who did not embrace that direction was not encouraged to stay. I was one of those who fell into that category.

I was left without a job, and our family was without a church home. We were very discouraged and were all asking, "Where were you, God?" The experience tested our faith. Some friends that we thought would support us never even made an effort to see how we were doing, but we do thank the Lord for those few who stood with us.

Over time, we had to work through the issue of forgiveness. Several years later, the pastor contacted us and asked for our forgiveness. This completed what God had already started in our hearts. We did forgive and were able to carry on and have a productive ministry.

We learned early on that forgiveness and grace are so necessary. As we obeyed the Scriptures, we were able to get through the painful situation. A question I often ask persecuted believers is, "Have you been able to forgive?" I am amazed at their responses. I continually hear how, despite the brutality committed against them or their loved ones, forgiveness is what has allowed them not to be bitter and full of hate. It is how they continue to be effective witnesses of Jesus. They have learned that the refusal to forgive, though justified from a worldly perspective, can be toxic, debilitating, and cause them to be ineffective for the kingdom of God.

That is not to say that they forget what happened. Rather, they put the situation in God's hands. The reality is that we cannot really forgive without God's help. That is been my personal experience as well as the experience of many I have met who have been persecuted for their faith. Our greatest example of forgiveness comes from our Lord Jesus Christ.

Jesus knew that those who crucified Him were blinded and filled with hate and anger. He chose to release those who were committing this barbaric act against Him to His Father, and He asked God to forgive them because they had no idea what they were doing (Luke 23:34). In that moment, Jesus gave His followers an example of what they were to do when they or their loved ones were unjustly treated, taken advantage of, lied about, physically harmed, or killed (1 Peter 2:21–23). Jesus' example is found in the life and martyrdom of one of the first deacons of the church.

In Acts 7, we read about Stephen delivering a fiery and emotionally charged speech to religious leaders after being dragged before the Sanhedrin on false charges of blasphemy. In his speech, Stephen took the Sanhedrin through some of the highlights of Israel's history and how they had rejected God and His prophets while resisting the Holy Spirit and murdering Jesus.

Soon, the religious leaders could not take it any longer, and their anger toward Stephen boiled over. The Bible says that they "cried out with a loud voice, stopped their ears, and ran at him with one accord" (Acts 7:57–58).

As they chased him out of the city and began to stone him, Stephen's response is nothing short of amazing. Instead of calling down God's judgment from heaven on these hate-filled people who were trying to kill him, he lifted up a prayer similar to what Jesus had expressed as He hung on the cross. Stephen cried out, "Lord, do not charge them with this sin" (Acts 7:60). Moments later, the early Church had its first martyr. Over the centuries, many followers of Jesus have uttered those same words —some while being attacked, others just before they died. For many, forgiveness was a process as they chose to obey Scripture over their emotions and desire for revenge. The following are some modern-day examples.

## Manini's Nightmare

Manini Digal has a beautiful smile. She is even able to look to the future with anticipation, which is quite remarkable. This sixteen-year-old girl from a Christian home endured a nightmare when Hindu militants went on a rampage in the villages of the Kandhamal District in Orissa State in the summer of 2008.

On an August afternoon that year, twenty-five to thirty Hindu militants came to her village and attacked a church. They burned homes and then went to the house where Manini and her family lived. She said her father went outside to try to reason with this angry mob, but they were in no mood for talking. They were bent on attacking Christians.

"They started to beat my father," Manini said, "and they were going to kill him but he was able to run away from our home. They then beat my grandfather and my mother. I was inside, being silent. Next they ran in the house, grabbed my hair, and started yelling at me. They said I was getting proud, so they dragged me outside and started to beat me with sticks all over my legs, arms, and head. My hands and legs weren't working so I couldn't escape," she recalled tearfully. "One man took out a knife to kill me, but then he put it back. Someone else took out a sword to kill me, and I saw that as he was going to hit me, the blade of the sword suddenly turned. I believe God protected me."

What makes this violent attack even worse is that two of Manini's assailants were fellow students from her school. She recognized two others from the village. She says the mob of boys and men ranged in age from fifteen to thirty. After she was beaten unconscious, Manini was also raped, though thankfully

*Manini's injured arm*

she has no memory of that. The brutal assault did not stop there. "They poured kerosene on me to burn me. During that time I was in very much pain," she said. "After they burned me, they left and went somewhere else. I got up. I'm not sure where I got the strength, but some strength came into me. I got up and ran to another house."

This horrendous situation was not over for Manini. As she ran for help, with her clothing ablaze, a Hindu began beating her with a stick. Manini was able to pour water on her body to extinguish the flames, but she was in excruciating pain. She described what happened as she struggled to get to a family member's house: "After I rescued myself, I was hiding in the house of a relative. Another man came and attacked my auntie, who is a Hindu, with a sword. He was looking for me to kill me, but couldn't find me. After that man left, I was trying to get help from somebody because my body was burned, and my auntie couldn't help me because she had been attacked. I just sat down." Her father soon found her, however, "and when he saw me he cried a lot," Manini continued. "Then he said, 'Let's go to the hospital.'"

The right side of Manini's body was severely burned, and she arrived at the village hospital in critical condition. The following day, Manini was taken by local officials to the government hospital, but even there she could not receive the care she needed. "Those who beat me came to the hospital and threatened the doctors, 'Don't keep her here; if you do, we will kill you.' I told my mother, 'I will never be able to stretch out my hand again; my hand will always be like this.' I was crying."

*"If I see them again, I won't be angry with them; I will talk with love."*

However, help would come from Christians in another part of the country where she would receive the proper medical treatment for her burns.

Manini was grateful to the Christians in India and around the world who were helping her by covering the medical costs for the surgeries. She said she has grown in her relationship with the Lord since the terrible events of August 2008. Because of that, she was able to forgive those who brutally attacked her and tried to take her life. "I have forgiven them because they don't know Jesus Christ. Because of that they did it, and I have forgiven them," said Manini. "If I see them again, I won't be angry with them; I will talk with love."

Manini choose the difficult path to forgive her persecutors, but forgiveness brings freedom. Because she forgave, she is not a bitter young lady wanting revenge but is instead a disciple of Jesus. "My future is with the Lord," Manini said, "and where He leads, I will go."

In 2011, Manini shared with a VOM worker about how her faith, despite the horrors she has faced, has grown since the attack. "I believe God can do impossible things for me," she said. "I believe now that He can do all things."

## Bukar Samson: Left for Dead

Bukar Samson's scarred face and body are the result of a brutal attack by militant Hausa-Fulani Muslims on February 24, 2004. The attack, which claimed the lives of dozens of Christians, took place in the town of Yelwa in Nigeria's Plateau State. Numerous buildings were burned and several churches were destroyed, including the church where Bukar's father was the pastor.

Plateau State is located in central Nigeria between the mostly Muslim north and the mostly Christian south. Although Christians and Muslims peacefully coexisted until 2001, attacks against believers have been increasing as Christianity spreads. According to Dr. Soja Bewarang, president of one of Nigeria's

*Bukar pointing to a scar*

largest evangelical denominations, the growing violence is due to "the expansion of Christianity from Plateau particularly, which is the centre of Christianity. All denominations are headquartered in Plateau." Just two weeks before I met with Dr. Bewarang, a suicide bomber with the Boko Haram had detonated a car bomb at his church, killing three members of the congregation—and it could have been much worse. According to Dr. Bewarang, "The denominations are serious about evangelism and reaching out in the Muslim north. Islam is beginning to see Christianity as a threat to its existence."

Bukar and other believers were gathered at their church for an early morning prayer service when their town was overrun by a frenzied group of militant Muslims, driven by hatred and bent on destroying their perceived enemies: the Christians.

"Islamic fanatics came into our church early in the morning," explained Bukar. "They surrounded us and they started cutting people. People were just running up and down, nowhere to escape." Both Bukar and his father were hit with a machete and were badly injured, and many other believers lay dying on the floor. As he was trying to stay alive in the midst of the chaos, Bukar was struck again with a machete. "When I was running to escape for my life, they ran toward me and hit me in the head. I fell into the midst of those dead people," he continued. "They thought I was a dead person because I was covered with blood. I kept lying down there."

Their church building was set ablaze, and the pastoral house and even the cars were set on fire. Bukar, a serious but passionate follower of Christ, said he was gripped by fear as he lay on the blood-soaked floor of his church. It was there he prayed to God, almost certain he was going to die. "The only thing I can do, I now surrender my life to Christ. I said I hand over everything under His care, either alive or dead, since He is the Creator. I have no other option," he told me.

Amazingly, Bukar escaped from the now smouldering church building. Once government soldiers arrived, he went back into the church to find his father still alive, though barely. The wounded were taken to the hospital, where Bukar's father later died. Bukar was seriously injured and had lost a lot of blood. According to Christian leaders in northern Nigeria, forty-eight believers were killed in that church attack, and countless others wounded. Another thirty to fifty Christians were killed in the village.

Bukar is grateful to the Lord for sparing his life. "It's only God who saved my life; He knows why He saved my life." Prior to his father's death, Bukar did not have any real interest in entering full-time ministry, but a few months later he sensed God's call to follow in the footsteps of his father and enter the pastorate. "God even talked to me one day that that is the right path I should follow. Some people were discouraging me, saying if I follow those footsteps, I know what happened to my late father. They said I shouldn't do that, but I didn't even listen to them." Bukar went to seminary and studied to be a pastor. His mother, Jemina, is very proud of her son. "I'm grateful my son has taken the first step to being a pastor," she stated. "What happened has happened for a purpose. God allowed my son not to die."

Bukar said he is able to forgive those who killed his father and took the lives of his friends and fellow Christians in Yelwa, but he admits it has not been easy. "When the incident took place, what came into my mind was that I will never forgive them. But when I keep on going through the Scripture, the Bible encourages me in one way or the other. I have now said I have forgiven them all for what they did. God should forgive them, because they don't know Christ; I believe that is why they are doing such things."

Bukar and Manini discovered the power in Jesus' words about forgiveness, and through faith they put those words into action—even after the horrible things that were done to them. As a result, they are free from hatred and are able to live their lives in love, rather than in bitterness and anger.

But what if those who wanted to kill you were people who are supposed to love you? That is exactly what happened to an Egyptian believer by the name of Mohammed Hegazy.

## Forgiving Your Family:
## Mohammed and Christina Hegazy

Mohammed Hegazy of Egypt was forced into hiding with his wife and daughter after he took the unprecedented step of going to court to change his religion on his national ID card. He was the first Egyptian Muslim convert to Christianity to seek official government recognition of his conversion. Although Christianity is legal in Egypt, and anyone can convert to Islam from another religion, it is not legal to leave Islam. Apostasy from Islam is punishable by death under a widespread interpretation of Islamic law. Killings are rare, however, and the state has never ordered or carried out an execution.

The story of Mohammed's desire to be legally recognized as a Christian was leaked to the press, igniting a firestorm of controversy that seemed to reach every major Arabic-speaking television station. His highly publicized case went to court, but the judge refused to acknowledge his right to change his religion to Christianity. Undeterred, Mohammed continued his legal fight to be officially recognized as a Christian.

*Mohammed Hegazy*

Despite the great risks, Mohammed felt compelled to change his ID card to accurately report his religion in order to set a precedent for other converts. He also wanted to ensure his children can openly be raised Christian, have a Christian name, and be able to marry in a church. Those would all be prohibited otherwise, because children are registered in the religion of their father.

After receiving numerous death threats, Mohammed was forced into hiding with his then pregnant wife, Christine, also a Muslim convert to Christ. A month later, baby Miriam was born. Christine's family has threatened to kill her because she not only married a Christian, but she left Islam—something that her family believes has brought disgrace on them. However, Christine said that has not stopped her from loving them. "I love my parents so much," she said. "I want them to know I'm praying that the Lord will open their hearts and minds, that He will show them the way and that they would get the same blessing that I'm getting"—the privilege of knowing God in a personal way through Jesus Christ.

Mohammed's family was just as angry as Christine's. In an interview with the local newspapers, Mohammed's father said, "I'm going to try to talk to my son and convince him to return to Islam; if he refuses, I'm going to kill him with my own hands." Shortly afterward, Mohammed released this response through the media: "I would like to send a message to my dad. I saw what you said in the newspaper. You say you want to shed my blood in public, but I love you so much because you are my dad and because Jesus taught me to love. I accepted Jesus Christ willingly; nobody forced me. I forgive you, no matter what decision you make, no matter what you do. To my dad and mom I say Jesus Christ died to save me."

*"You say you want to shed my blood in public, but I love you so much … because Jesus taught me to love."*

Following Jesus was a costly decision, but one Mohammed made in 1998 when he was sixteen. His journey toward Jesus began after he started doing comparative studies in religions, explaining that the major issue for him was love: "Islam wasn't promoting love as Christianity did." His new faith in Jesus was tested early and often. When his father learned of his conversion, he called the State Security, and Mohammed was arrested and questioned by a very aggressive officer. "His questions were about 'who helped you to embrace Christianity?' and he wanted to know names of the people," Mohammed explained. "But I told him my testimony about how I listened to the Christian radio station, and that nobody helped me to become a Christian. So he spent three days torturing me in a very serious way, a very rough way. He was beating me, he was whipping me, and he was putting his shoes into my face."

According to Mohammed, there is a specialized office in the State Security to investigate Christian evangelism. "All the officers in that office are really fanatic about their Islam, really religious. They are very tough and severe against the Muslim converts to Christianity and the Christians," Mohammed said, adding that one of the officers became more vicious as he beat him. "This officer was praying and taking more energy to torture me. Others also beat me. They put a blindfold over my eyes so I couldn't see where I would be beaten."

Mohammed was confused by what was happening to him. "I couldn't understand my crime, why they were doing that to me, just because I was a Christian. After three days, the officer brought in a Muslim scholar who tried to convince me to return to Islam, and I told him I didn't need anyone to convince me because I was a Christian."

Despite death threats, torture, and imprisonment, Mohammed has stayed true to Christ. "I've been arrested dozens of times; I can't remember how many times. A few days each time, once for two months—sometimes they would torture me, and sometimes they wouldn't even ask me questions," he said. "Many Muslim scholars issued a *Fatwa* [death sentence] saying I must be killed. On television, people were saying if they meet me on the streets they will kill me. Many *Fatwas* have been issued saying I must be killed."

Mohammed told me that God has protected him and his family many times, and he is determined to love those who want to harm him and his family. He continues to forgive those who do not know what they are doing, even those who raised him. In the meantime, he will continue to share his faith and serve the Lord in whatever way he can.

## OUR CHALLENGE: FORGIVING IN JESUS' NAME

Before going into ministry I worked as a sports reporter, and I often interviewed players from both the winning and losing teams after a game to get their perspective on what happened. The answers were fairly predictable: if they won, credit was given to their teammates; and if they lost, the players would try to explain what they did not do right in the game. It was almost like they had a manual on how to answer the questions in a proper way.

Likewise, in my years of interviewing persecuted Christians, I have discovered that many of them give similar answers to my questions. They, too, have a Manual on how to respond in the proper way. However, unlike the athletes, Christians like Manini, Bukar, Mohammed, and Christine gave their heartfelt answers based on what they learned from God's Word. What the Bible tells us is the right perspective is what they truly believe. I have observed that those who are passionate in their relationship with Jesus Christ, regardless of where they live in the world, say much the same things because they are reading and meditating on the same Book. They can genuinely respond with forgiveness because that is what their Manual says they must do.

This side of heaven, we all will have countless choices to forgive or to grow bitter. For some of us, the little things that we do not consider significant enough to "forgive" can add up, gradually hardening our heart so that we have difficulty forgiving. Many others have experienced a traumatic event or personal tragedy that makes unforgiveness seem a natural choice.

We all have excuses not to forgive. *They aren't going to pay if I forgive.* But how does your refusal to forgive them make them pay? Turn them over to God; He is the one who will avenge (Romans 12:19). *I can't trust them, so I can't forgive them.* Trust and forgiveness are two separate issues. Forgiveness has to do with our relationship with God. If we do not forgive others, God will not forgive us (Matthew 6:15). We all need to be forgiven. Trust, on the other hand, needs to be earned. You can forgive someone and not put yourself in a position to be hurt or victimized again. *They need to ask for forgiveness before I can forgive them.* Read Jesus' parable of the unmerciful servant in Matthew 18:21–35 to see why waiting for a person to ask for forgiveness is a bad idea.

Like Manini, Bukar, Mohammed, and Christine, we need to forgive. Christ's example on the cross is the last word for His followers. We cannot choose the path of bitterness. Too much is at stake!

## CONSIDER & SHARE

- As you read the accounts of the individuals in this chapter, did you remember an offence you need to forgive? Take a moment now and ask the Holy Spirit to show you if there are any. Then ask Him to help you forgive them from the heart.

- Have you had to forgive someone of a significant offence? To forgive does not mean to forget, nor does it condone the offence. When you remember the offence, remember you have forgiven.

- Can you talk about your experience without speaking badly of the person who offended you? Can you do as Jesus said to do in Matthew 5:44, and pray for that person? By faith, do this today, because others will learn from your example.

# CHAPTER 4

# FROM PERSECUTOR TO PERSECUTED

*"And [Saul] said, 'Who are You, Lord?' Then the
Lord said, 'I am Jesus, whom you are persecuting.'"*
ACTS 9:5

Have you ever wanted God to "just take care" of someone
who did you wrong? We have assurances throughout
Scripture that God will judge fairly. In the book of Revelation,
those who were slain cried out from under the altar, "How
long, O Lord, holy and true, until You judge and avenge our
blood on those who dwell on the earth?" (6:10). We take comfort in knowing that He is a righteous judge, and He will act
justly.

I hope you caught that juxtaposition. On the one hand, we
need to forgive those who have committed an offence against
us. On the other, we need to leave them to God, knowing He
will avenge. Our part is to turn it over to God and let Him
judge. This allows us to lift up prayers like the ones I hear
from the persecuted Church. One prayer I have heard many
times in my travels goes something like this: "Lord, take those
who are persecuting Your Church and make them like Paul."

You know the story of a man named Saul, who hated and
persecuted the followers of Jesus until one day the Lord Himself
confronted him on the road to Damascus (Acts 9). The resur-

rected Jesus made it clear to Saul that in persecuting those who are the Body of Christ, he was persecuting the Lord Himself. It was not long before Saul was transformed into Paul, who worked to expand the Church more aggressively than he had worked to destroy it.

The believers you will meet in this chapter have a lot in common with this early church leader and writer of much of the New Testament. Keder from Ethiopia and Neeladri from India were enemies of the Church until something supernatural occurred. As their stories remind us, our God who we see at work through the Church in the book of Acts is still at work in His Church today.

## Keder: From Thief to Evangelist

Keder Danabew is an evangelist and former Muslim who faces constant danger in the East African nation of Ethiopia. He has been beaten, tortured, and imprisoned since coming to Christ in 1996. Keder was a notorious thief prior to becoming a Christian. He often beat his wife, and his hatred toward Christians was well known. But God worked in his life in a very powerful way, and Keder told me how Jesus appeared to him not once, but twice.

*Keder, showing how attackers placed a sword at his throat*

The first occasion took place during the Muslim evening prayer time. According to Keder, he was overwhelmed to see Jesus standing right in front of him as he was praying to Allah. Confused and shocked by what had happened, he went and told his wife, "Meseret," a Christian. While she was excited and overjoyed, Keder was not. He felt this was an evil attack and that his wife was somehow mocking him, so he started to beat her. Some neighbours heard her screams and intervened. Moments later, Keder said, Jesus appeared to him again and told him to follow Him, which he knew he had to do. Bewildered, he suddenly walked out, leaving his wife and neighbours wondering what was going on.

Keder said he followed Jesus, who took him through the town and across a bridge to a local church. It was a Sunday morning and the service was already underway. Keder's sudden appearance at the church interrupted the worship service. The people there were suspicious about why he had come and if he was there to cause trouble, since this well-known thief had a history of hostility toward Christians.

"The church leaders called me to the pulpit," Keder told me, "and they said, 'We worship the Jesus you persecuted, that you hate.' They asked, 'What is the reason for you coming?' and I said, 'It was Jesus who brought me here, the same Jesus that you worship.'"

The church leaders then asked Keder if he was willing to repent of his sins and follow Jesus. Keder—who by now understood that Jesus appearing to him was not an evil attack, but was from God—said yes, adding, "I accepted Jesus Christ at that moment." While his understanding of sin, repentance, and forgiveness would deepen in the days ahead, he realized that Jesus could help him.

Keder, then thirty-two years old, knew his decision to follow Christ would mean persecution and hardship—after all, he had been one to persecute Christians. Just four days after he trusted Christ, some Muslims in his village heard of his conversion and tried to force him to convert back to Islam. "They tied my hands and threatened me with a sword," he said of his attackers. "They were beating and torturing me. I was saying to them, 'If I die here in this place, then a church will be built here...'" Even as a new believer, Keder seemed to understand being a martyr for Christ. He survived that attack and many others that followed, which have left scars all over his body.

Right after his conversion, Keder started sharing his testimony of how he became a follower of Jesus and the amazing things the Lord did in his life, and this was the beginning of his ministry as an evangelist. Some of the people in his village responded to the gospel and became Christians. That further enraged some members of the Islamic community, who burned down his house and destroyed his fields in an effort to intimidate him. Local Christians, who had seen the transformation in Keder's life, helped support him and his family. Keder was a frequent target of the militant Muslims, and there would be more beatings, torture, and intimidation—not only for him, but also for those he led to the Lord.

Keder said his family also suffered because of his work as an evangelist. After finding a new home, Keder said, "The Muslims tried to burn our house and burn my wife and daughter alive." But the Lord protected them. On another occasion the militants cut his throat. In spite of all that has happened to him, Keder is grateful that the Lord intervened in his life and brought him into His kingdom, and he is willing to suffer for Jesus. He has a passion to tell others—even in a strong Muslim area—about how the Son of God can change lives!

## Neeladri: To Be a Witness Like Paul

Like Keder, Neeladri Kahanr went from persecuting Christians to being a persecuted Christian. For most of his life, Neeladri, a husband and father of six, hated Christians, because he saw them as enemies in his desire that India become a Hindu-only country. Neeladri joined the militant Hindutva group that was responsible for attacks against the followers of Christ in Orissa State, India. "I was the main leader among the Hindus in my village of Tellapale," he told me. "This organization started in 1980. We were taught that Christians were mistreating all the Hindu people and were putting cows in the wells. [Cows are

treated with reverence in Hinduism.] So I was told to organ-
ize people and stand for my
religion. I organized people to
beat Christians."

His hatred for Christians
came to an abrupt halt in 2005.
One of Neeladri's young daughters was gravely ill, and with
doctors in the area unable to
help, the family was desperate.
They sought the help of local
pastor Potitra Mohan Katta,
who not only shared the gospel with the family but prayed

*Neeladri kneeling*

for the sick girl. It wasn't long before the little girl recovered.
Amazed by the healing, and by the power of God, Neeladri
and his family surrendered their lives to Christ.

When the militant Hindus found out about his conversion
to Christianity, Neeladri became a target. He received death
threats and beatings. The worst incident took place on August
27, 2008, when his village was attacked by a Hindu mob.

Neeladri was with his youngest daughter, going to the store
to get food. Suddenly the two were surrounded by people with
knives and swords, yelling, "Catch him! Catch him!" The mob
had no interest in the girl, so she was able to run home and tell
her mother that her father was in trouble. As Neeladri tried to
escape, the mob began throwing rocks at him.

"I was afraid and just bowed down to Jesus and said, 'Lord
I surrender myself.' When I bowed my head," Neeladri recalled, "someone came and hit me in the head. I fell down and
someone came with a sword to chop me, but another person
said, 'It's not good to spill his blood here.' So they beat me with
sticks and iron rods for half an hour. They thought I was dead
and left."

After learning that her husband had been caught by a mob, Neeladri's wife went looking for him. She saw from a distance that he was lying on the ground as another group of men came by and beat him some more. She reported that four people urinated on his face, then three people took poison from a tree and put it on his eyes. The actions of these men, who believed Neeladri had been killed, were intended to desecrate the body of this Christian convert.

Eventually, Neeladri's wife came to what she thought was her husband's dead body. "My wife also thought I was dead and brought a cloth to cover my body," Neeladri explained. Even the local newspaper reported the next day that Neeladri had been killed in the attacks on the village. He lay motionless for several hours, and then he suddenly regained consciousness.

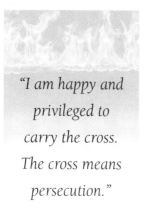

*"I am happy and privileged to carry the cross. The cross means persecution."*

"My leg wasn't functioning. My hand wasn't functioning. I was trying to get up. I was hungry. No one was there to give me food," Neeladri said. "Then I heard a voice say, 'Men shall not live by bread alone, but by the Word of God.'"

At that time God spoke to his wife and told her to go to Neeladri because life had returned to him. "She thought I was already dead, so she was afraid, and was standing a long distance away and calling to me asking if I was alive." Neeladri called back to his wife that he was still alive, and she was overjoyed! Although the beatings left Neeladri badly injured, he is grateful to have suffered no permanent damage to his body or eyes.

As you would expect, this event has profoundly affected his life. Neeladri is more determined to serve Jesus, and has a strong desire to see many come to know the Saviour, no matter what the cost. He told me, "When he was discipling me, my pastor said, 'If you go after Jesus, then you must carry the cross.' I am happy and privileged to carry the cross. The cross means persecution."

Neeladri has little doubt about why the Lord spared his life, and he says, "I believe God has raised me up so I can be a mighty witness for Him like Paul."

## OUR CHALLENGE: PRAYING FOR OUR ENEMIES

Both Keder and Neeladri did an incredible about-face. Not only were their eternal destinies changed, but also the destinies of their families, as well as those who have come to Christ as a result of their powerful testimonies. The men went from fighting against God to becoming fearless disciples of Jesus! The Lord has been doing this kind of transformation in the building of His Church for two thousand years, and the men featured in this chapter are just two of many.

A question I used to ask myself when I talked to people like Keder and Neeladri—and maybe it is something you have wondered about—is: Why does God sometimes intervene and sometimes not appear? I have come to a point where I know I probably will not get the answer to questions like that. All I know is that our Lord is sovereign, and it is His kingdom; He can and will do things His way. I am constantly reminded that His ways are much higher than the ways of man, yet He chooses to make us a part of His plan. So, while I still may ask questions from time to time about why He works the way He does, I am more content with not needing an answer. I am just glad God is working to bring others to Himself, and that stories like the jaw-dropping accounts in the book of Acts are still taking place today. I pray that stories such as these will build up your faith, as they have mine.

There is a compelling story from Israel's history that demonstrates how God can use us to shake up the enemy's camp. At the time, Israel's army had no swords, but the Philistines had the technology for iron working and thus controlled the region with swords. With great faith in God to deliver them, Jonathan, King Saul's son, performed a daring attack against the Philistines with his armourbearer. The news of their successful offensive quickly spread, and God then caused an earthquake sending the Philistines into a panic. As the enemy's army began to run, something else amazing happened:

> Moreover the Hebrews who were with the Philistines before that time, who went up with them into the camp from the surrounding country, they also joined the Israelites who were with Saul and Jonathan. Likewise all the men of Israel who had hidden in the mountains of Ephraim, when they heard that the Philistines fled, they also followed hard after them in the battle. (1 Samuel 14:21,22)

All of us know people who are "hiding in the hills" and are not on the front-lines of what God is doing. Some of us even know people who have "gone over to the enemy" and are actively fighting against God's people. We can and should pray for a Damascus Road experience for them, but I want to challenge you even further.

The story started with Jonathan saying, "It may be that the LORD will work for us. For nothing restrains the LORD from saving by many or by few" (1 Samuel 14:6). He was acting on an order God had given Joshua to rid the land of tribes whose sin had reached its full measure (Genesis 15:16). Joshua did not complete the order, so it was a standing order for all who followed. We each have a standing order, too: to love God with all our heart, soul, mind, and strength and to love our neighbours as ourselves (Luke 10:27). Jonathan did something crazy and daring. He did not sneak up. He gave up the high ground. He and his armourbearer were just two against an entire outpost. It was not the smartest tactical thing to do, but he did it and God provided the earthquake.

Pray for people who are actively working against God. Pray they will have an encounter with Jesus like Saul did on the way to Damascus. Also, consider how you can radically show God's love to others. Do it in the open—don't sneak in. Give up the high ground—be willing to be vulnerable with others, and let God worry about defending you. Do not wait for a crowd to go with you—God can use just you, since "nothing restrains the LORD from saving by few," or even by one. If you radically display God's love to the enemy, who knows? Perhaps God will do something amazing on your behalf, and those fellow soldiers hiding in the hills will join you in the battle, while those actively fighting against you will turn and work for God.

All I know is that the more I love, the more opportunity I give God to shake the ground around me.

Neeladri and those around him believe he died that fateful day in India and came back to life. But Neeladri was already dead before he was so brutally beaten. When he came to faith in Jesus Christ, he gave up his life—and so did we. Remember what Paul wrote to the Galatian believers? "I have been crucified with Christ; it is no longer I who live, but Christ lives in me" (Galatians 2:20).

Neeladri and Keder have had the privilege of being used to bring light into darkness, and while our own stories may not be as dramatic, there is still much rejoicing in the heavenlies when just one person repents (Luke 15:7,10). Neeladri's and Keder's testimonies give us hope to pray that the enemies we face in our lives will come to Christ, too.

 CONSIDER & SHARE

- Are you praying specifically for people who are working against God? Pray for their salvation and for God's blessing on them, remembering that we are to bless those who curse us (Matthew 5:44).

- Read Romans 12:20. How are you showing God's love to others—not just to family and friends, but especially to neighbours and strangers? Will they see Jesus in you today?

- Like with the example in 1 Samuel, some people need to see God at work before they are willing to step out and join the battle. By sharing these stories of spiritual victories with others, who can you encourage to join you on the front-lines?

# CHAPTER 5

# WORKING ALL THINGS TOGETHER FOR GOOD

*"And we know that all things work together for good to those who love God, to those who are the called according to His purpose."*

ROMANS 8:28

As a new Christian in the 1980s, one of the first verses I committed to memory was Romans 8:28. Who would not take comfort in knowing that "all things work together for good" in God's economy? I never imagined that I would use that Scripture one day to write about terrible events that God used for good. I know God is not to blame for these horrible things done to His followers, but I also know that what the enemy meant for evil God means for good (Genesis 50:20). I have seen God unexpectedly bring good things out of bad in my own life.

My experience is not as dramatic as the stories you will read in this chapter, but it provides another example of how our Lord has things under control even when we do not see it at the time.

It was January 2000, and I was on my first trip to Africa. Our destination was Sudan (now called South Sudan), where massive persecution of Christians had been ongoing for years. Approximately two million Sudanese had been killed, millions more were displaced, and thousands had been abducted and abused by Sudan's army. Oil and religion fed into the genocide as the Islamic-controlled government sought to impose Shariah (Islamic) law on the entire country, and bring the oil-rich south, dominated by Christians, under its control. The result was a long and brutal war.

Our trip to Sudan was interrupted when we arrived in Addis Ababa, Ethiopia, and our VOM team was informed that the border to Sudan had been closed. We were not able to enter directly into Sudan because of a regional war, and were forced to wait, pray, and find another way to get to Sudan. It took three days to be able to arrange for flights that would take us back to Nairobi, Kenya, and from there to the south Sudan border.

At the time, it seemed like a few wasted days in Addis Ababa were unavoidable. However, unknown to us, the Lord was orchestrating what would turn out to be significant meetings during that time.

Soon after arriving in Addis Ababa, our contacts put us in touch with "Joshua," who had grown up with a love for the persecuted Church. He introduced us to some young ladies who had been thrown out of their homes for embracing Jesus Christ, and I conducted my first interviews for The Voice of the Martyrs with them. Joshua, it turned out, had just finished Bible school training a few days earlier and was praying for the Lord's direction in ministry. A partnership soon began between Joshua and VOM Canada, which led to significant opportunities for VOM to minister not only in Ethiopia, but also in other East African nations.

Had we not been interrupted in our journey to Sudan, Ethiopia would have been just a quick stopover. The ministry in Sudan was not negatively impacted by the delay. In fact, it was a very productive and fruitful time. We were able to deliver blankets and hold a pastors' conference, which was a great success. I often remind myself of that unexpected stay in Ethiopia as one of those "all things" that work together for good when we are following Jesus Christ. God orchestrated out of that minor delay an amazing ministry for many years in Ethiopia, in which our brothers and sisters in Christ were helped and encouraged!

## Johannes: Scars for Jesus

Another example of God working "all things together for good" is the story of Johannes Mantahari of Indonesia. We interviewed him on the island of Sulawesi, while sitting on a dock over the still waters of Lake Poso, the village of Tentena in the background. What he said to us that day was powerful.

Johannes is from the Maluku Islands in the eastern part of the country. In the late 1990s, militant Muslims had attacked Christians in his village, with five hundred jihadists showing up to cause death and destruction. The Christians were greatly outnumbered and fearful, so they attempted to flee. Some managed to get away, but others did not— including Johannes, who was nineteen at the time.

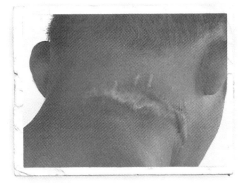

*Johannes' scars*

Several jihadists caught up with him and threatened that if he did not become a Muslim they would kill him. Johannes informed his captors that he did not want to convert to Islam and said, "Just kill me. I will accept that."

One of the jihadists struck Johannes's ear with a samurai sword. They continued wildly swinging their swords as they sliced into his back, left shoulder, forearm, and the back of his neck, nearly severing Johannes' head from his body. In desperation, Johannes did the only thing he could think of: he prayed. As he cried out to the Lord for help, his attackers mockingly asked, "Why do you shout to the Lord? Your Lord cannot save you from us!"

Following the brutal attack, the Muslims covered Johannes' bloodied, badly injured body with banana leaves and tried to light them on fire. But the leaves were too green and would not burn. In their frustration, the jihadists struck him again with a sword, hitting Johannes in the back and legs. Miraculously, he felt no pain. After his attackers left him to die, he was able to crawl to safety, inching his way along the ground until he found a cave where he could rest temporarily.

Severely wounded, Johannes stumbled through the jungle for eight days crying out for help. He was finally discovered by his brother-in-law who, along with some family and friends, had been searching the jungle for Johannes. They rejoiced to find him alive and rushed him to the hospital for treatment. Johannes lost a lot of blood and should have died, but he believes it was a miracle he survived. "While I lay weak and bleeding in the jungle, I prayed to God saying I could not bear this trial anymore," Johannes told us. "I begged Him to take my life, but I felt Him telling me this is not my time to leave this world."

Johannes views the scars on his body as badges of honour for Jesus. Knowing how much he had been personally forgiven by the Lord, he says he is able to forgive his attackers as our Father in heaven forgives us. He takes seriously Jesus' words in Matthew 6:15: "But if you do not forgive men their trespasses, neither will your Father forgive your trespasses."

What he told our team as we interviewed him caused us to listen very carefully. Johannes said his suffering has made him a much stronger, more committed follower of Jesus and that this spiritual growth has given him hope for the future. "I believe God allowed all this to happen to me because He wanted to change my life and use me for His purposes. Before this happened, I never dreamed I'd be an evangelist. Now I want to be a missionary to the people of Halmahera" (the largest island in Indonesia's Maluku Islands). He has since attended Bible school, where he studied evangelism, then joined a medical missions team to help provide urgent care for Indonesians in remote areas.

"I pray for my attackers that God will bless them," said Johannes. "I want to see them again. I will thank them for attacking me and tell them that because of them, I've become closer to God." How many of us would say the same?

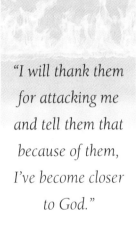

*"I will thank them for attacking me and tell them that because of them, I've become closer to God."*

When the apostle Paul wrote that "all things work together for good," he specified that it was "to those who love God, to those who are the called according to His purpose." We may not understand it, but we can just trust that God has a purpose even in our suffering. I know that when I go through difficult situations and can see no value in them, I am often reminded of the powerful testimony of Johannes. He more than memorized a verse; he embedded it in his heart. You and I need to do the same, regardless of the situations we face.

## Lalani: "I Will Stay"

Can the murder of your spouse be one of those "all things" that God uses for good? Can anything good come out of the violent death of a loved one?

I met Lalani Jayasinghe after a long day of driving to what was almost the southernmost point on the island nation of Sri Lanka. I was exhausted, hungry, not in the best of moods, and ready to fall into bed when we finally arrived at the church.

*Lalani Jayasinghe*

The sun was starting to set as we were greeted by this friendly and humble woman of God.

Lalani gives pastoral leadership to a growing evangelical church in the town of Tissamaharama. Many in her congregation are enduring difficulty and persecution because of their devotion to Jesus in what is known as the oldest continually Buddhist country. Yet Lalani is very effective in encouraging Christians facing persecution to be strong in their faith because her own faith in God has been severely tested.

She believes the Lord prepared her for what would be the biggest challenge of her life. In 1988, her thirty-eight-year-old husband, Lionel, an ex-Buddhist monk, was leading a vibrant church, and they had an eleven-month-old son, Shamger. "We had fasting and prayer with our workers," she explained. "In the morning, my husband said, 'I have a feeling I will die soon.' I told him, 'God is going to give me strength.' In the evening, we went for visitations and returned home joyful. Later my husband and I were together, and I heard our son cry. I went to his bedroom. He was walking for the first time in his life, so I called out, 'Pastor, Pastor, your son is walking.' He came in and the last words he uttered to his son were, 'My brave son.'"

Suddenly there was a knock at the door. Lionel went to greet their visitors, leaving his wife and toddler son in the bedroom. Moments later Lalani heard a gunshot. Lionel staggered into the bedroom pursued by his attackers. Lalani was horrified to see he had been shot in the face. As she watched helplessly, the two men stabbed Lionel in the back and shot him again. They were contract killers, sent by Buddhists angry over his Christian activity in the village and surrounding area.

After the assassins fled, leaving Lionel badly wounded and near death, Lalani rushed him to the hospital. Lionel died before they arrived.

At the hospital, a devastated Lalani touched her husband's lifeless legs and prayed to the Lord. With tears streaming down her face as she recalled that night, she shared with us her heartfelt prayer: "I will never leave this area for two reasons," she told the Lord. "You started this ministry with my husband here, and I want to continue the ministry. I want to look after these new believers who were converted from Buddhist families. I can't abandon them. So I will be staying here."

The night Lionel was murdered, Lalani immediately told God she forgave those who took her husband from her. Upon returning home, she remembered the words of Job, and said, "Lord, You have given and You have taken, but praise be to You."

Shortly after Lionel's funeral, Lalani and Shamger were evicted from their rented home because people in the village had pressured the landlord. The mother and child moved to a new location in the village but their troubles and hardships continued. Lalani, who had taken over the pastoral role following her husband's death, was active in evangelism and as a result Buddhists and other villagers were coming to Christ. She was also teaching her congregation to share their faith with others. Lalani received many death threats from those opposed to Christianity, and their house, which was also used as a meeting place for the church, was stoned and damaged a number of times.

A few months later, Lalani's congregation bought a piece of land to construct a church building of their own, and the opposition was fierce right from the beginning. Some of the believers were beaten and assaulted; Bibles and books were confiscated and burned. Eventually they were able to finish the church building. Over the next eleven years, the Christians in the village still were under pressure not knowing when they might next be attacked. Things took a violent turn on April 2, 1999 (Good Friday), when the church was bombed and badly damaged.

At the time we visited, Lalani had planted seven churches, five of which have their own buildings. And while there have not been any attacks on the church buildings in recent years, problems continue for the pastors under Lalani's leadership. They are harassed, beaten, and threatened with death, but she instructs them to keep an eternal perspective and reminds them that those who persecute Christians need to know Jesus.

*"If they die they will go to hell without knowing Him, but if you die, you will go to heaven."*

"I love these people," she says of their persecutors, "and I know if I die today I will go to heaven and be with my Lord. I'm encouraging my believers and telling them, 'You better love the people. If they die they will go to hell without knowing Him, but if you die, you will go to heaven.' I'm encouraging them to do that. No matter what happens here, we have eternal life."

Lalani's ministry is strong because of her strong faith—a faith that is been tested many times. Though she has "been grieved by various trials," she can rejoice that "the genuineness of [her] faith, being much more precious than gold that perishes, though it is tested by fire, may be found to praise, honour, and glory at the revelation of Jesus Christ" (1 Peter 1:6,7). This confident woman of God is a wonderful example of how the Lord takes what was meant for evil—the brutal and senseless death of her husband, a man committed to God and His kingdom—and turns it into something good.

Another believer who refused to give in to bitterness against those who tried to stop the work of the Lord in his life is Richard

Wurmbrand, founder of The Voice of the Martyrs. He did not let torture and fourteen years of imprisonment (including three years in solitary confinement) destroy him. Pastor Wurmbrand became so effective in his ministry to the persecuted Church because he discovered that what was meant for evil could actually be used for good, and could even give him compassion instead of hatred for those who persecuted him. The same is true for other followers of Jesus who suffer for their faith. Like Pastor Wurmbrand, Lalani and Johannes learned that some of the "all things," even the terrible things, can be used for good in God's kingdom.

## OUR CHALLENGE: TRUSTING GOD IN ALL THINGS

Our God is always working in our circumstances, even when we do not realize it. We must keep in mind that He is more committed to His kingdom than we are, and that He has chosen to work with us and through us to accomplish His will. It is often tough to remember that while we are in the middle of a crisis—until we take our eyes off the circumstances and focus on our all-powerful God. Seeing how He has worked in the lives of Johannes and Lalani to turn terrible things into good should give us confidence that He will do the same for us.

Next time you are in a difficult situation, remember: He has not forgotten you. He is not angry with you. He is not incapable of action. Trust Him. He is working all things together for good to those who love Him.

## CONSIDER & SHARE

- When you have gone through terrible circumstances, was it difficult to believe that God was going to work all things together for good? Explain.

- Read 2 Corinthians 1:3–6. What was something that encouraged you when you went through difficult times? Can you think of someone else you can encourage with what encouraged you?

- Is there any circumstance you are currently experiencing that seems impossible for you to get though? Find Scriptures that speak of God's promises for believers and pray through them to God. You will be agreeing with Him for your future. Some verses to consider include Zechariah 4:6; John 16:33; Romans 8:32–37; 1 John 4:4; 5:4; Revelation 3:21; 12:11.

# CHAPTER 6

# JESUS DIVIDES EVEN FAMILIES

*"Do not think that I came to bring peace on earth. I did not come to bring peace but a sword. For I have come to 'set a man against his father, a daughter against her mother, and a daughter-in-law against her mother-in-law'; and 'a man's enemies will be those of his own household.'"*

MATTHEW 10:34–36

When I came to Christ at the age of twenty-three, several people in my life likely thought I was a little too intense. Right from the start, I was passionate about my faith in Jesus! I saw life in a whole new way and I was excited to find out what God had in store for me.

Naturally, after I became a Christian, my lifestyle changed. I was no longer interested in going to bars and parties. I avoided crude conversations and coarse jokes. I felt like an outsider at times with some of my coworkers and friends who were not Christians. And at work as a broadcaster I had to make ethical decisions that sometimes put me in conflict with my bosses and coworkers.

Five years later, when I announced I was leaving my sports broadcasting career to attend Bible college and enter full-time ministry, I knew some people thought I was getting "too religious." My career was going really well. I was experienced and moving up in the broadcasting world, where I had some notoriety for anchoring on the supper-time newscast on a local television station. People in Edmonton and the surrounding area recognized me. Leaving sports broadcasting may not have seemed like the "rational" thing to do, to those who did not understand my reasons. Some may have seen me as being passionate for Jesus, but others may have wondered, *Why is he doing that?* When I told my parents that, with two small children at home, I would be quitting my job and going to Bible school, they did not say much. After all, I was making a good living in broadcasting and would soon have no income to support my family. Was I being irresponsible? Years later I learned they were very concerned, and, to be honest, I understand that.

I realized many people did not agree with or support my choices as a follower of Christ, and some of the responses were negative. There is often a spiritual reaction in those around us when we walk a kingdom lifestyle, and these reactions may come even from fellow believers and those who are close to us. For many persecuted Christians, however, the consequences of the division brought on by following Christ can be far more painful and devastating.

## Rachel: "I Never Expected the Suffering"

"Rachel" knows very well what Jesus meant when He said that if you follow Him, even members of your own family may turn against you. She had no idea just how high the cost would be when she became interested in Jesus as a teenager in Indonesia.

"When I was in junior high school," Rachel explained, "one of my Christian friends shared Jesus Christ with me and said through Him is the only way a person can get salvation."

Rachel wanted to hear more about Jesus but she was not thinking about becoming a Christian; she was just curious. Then one night she had a dream about Jesus being the Way and the Truth. "After the dream," she said, "I started to ask my Muslim friends and Muslim leaders about it. No one knew where the phrase came from, so I visited my aunt who was a Christian, and she showed me where it was in the Bible."

Rachel would have more questions for her aunt in the following weeks and, after coming to an understanding that Jesus died for her sins, she decided

"Rachel"

to become a Christian and be baptized in 2001 at the age of thirteen. She learned how to pray and read the Bible, but Rachel kept her new faith a secret from her Muslim family. This would change in 2004, when, only a month into high school, she boldly removed her Muslim head veil and openly declared her faith in Jesus. Shortly after that her faith would be tested. "When my family discovered I had become a Christian," she said, "many of my relatives and Muslims leaders came to my house to try to 'take the spell off of me.' They stretched my arms and said Arabic words and touched my head."

Rachel's uncle, a Muslim leader, said he talked about Islam with a man who claimed to be a Christian and the man became a Muslim, but he could not understand how a Muslim could become a Christian—especially one who was a member of his own family. How could she reject Islam? He and the rest of the family were very angry with Rachel and said she brought disgrace to the family by leaving Islam; she was now considered an infidel and should die.

Rachel was told that she was no longer a part of her family and that she could stay only if she returned to Islam. However, that was something she was not going to do. Rachel was determined to follow her Saviour. As a result, the sixteen-year-old was driven from her home. Of her family members, only her mother tried to intervene. Rachel said, "I was just crying, and I never thought this would happen to me. I never expected the suffering would come to me because of following Jesus."

Desperate and with nowhere to live, Rachel went to the pastor who had helped lead her to Christ, and he and his family took her in. The Voice of the Martyrs helped her start a small business where she sold cakes to pay her school fees so that she could continue her education. Rachel said she endured a lot because of her decision to leave Islam and follow Jesus Christ, but the decision has been worth it.

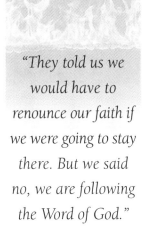

*"They told us we would have to renounce our faith if we were going to stay there. But we said no, we are following the Word of God."*

Still, being separated from her family for years has been painful and discouraging. She said, "At that time I prayed, 'You know, Lord, that I don't have biological parents, but I pray to You that if I need something, You always provide my needs.'" Rachel eventually had some contact with her family. While their hostility has subsided somewhat, they are still trying to convince her to return to Islam. "I pray to the Lord that if one member of my family is saved, I believe that all members of my family will be saved," she said unwavering. "I hold on to that promise."

When I met Rachel, she was training at an underground Bible discipleship school. Her passion is to reach Muslims and her family with the gospel. "In this training, I'm learning about contextual ministry," she explained. "We learn about local religions and local cultures. It's about reaching people through their religion—for example, reaching Muslims through the Qur'an. I have a dream to reach my tribe where most of them are Muslims." Rachel desires for her family to become Christians as well, so they, too, will experience the joy of knowing Jesus Christ and have the same love for Him that she does.

## Chiapas, Mexico: Expelled and Banned

It is not only families that are separated for following Christ. Sometimes the entire community, including relatives, will turn on those who have decided to follow Jesus instead of the local religion. A good example of that is what I discovered in Chiapas, Mexico.

Mexico is a secular state that offers citizens freedom of conscience as well as freedom of religion. Yet persecution of evangelicals occurs in certain parts of Mexico. In the southern states —particularly Chiapas, Oaxaca, and Guerrero—believers face prejudice, harassment, evictions, and vandalism of their churches and homes. This mostly occurs due to believers' refusal to participate in community religious events that involve traditional Christo-pagan practices.

On a cool night in San Cristobal in Chiapas, a family warms up around a fire in a refugee centre. Sebastian and Julia Hernandez, along with their children and grandchildren, were placed here by the government after being expelled from their community. They lost their house, small farm, and crops in Chilil, Huixtan, because of their evangelical Christian faith. Sebastian said, "There was a meeting of the local authorities, and they finally had us come in and talk to them and told us we would have to renounce our faith if we were going to stay there, and that people who did not practice the majority religion were not welcome there. But we said no, we are

*Julia Hernandez*

following the Word of God." Sebastian's family and another family would not renounce their faith in Christ and were ex-

81

pelled. Two other families did recant and were able to stay in the community.

Julia explained what happened when she was confronted by some of the villagers because of her stand for Christ. She said, "For several hours they tried to get me to renounce my faith, and I told them, 'I'm a Christian, I'm a Christian,' and I was not willing to renounce my faith." One of Julia's daughters witnessed her mother being dragged fifty metres. Julia said, "The police were pushing and shoving me and grabbed my arm, pulled me around, shouted at me and told me to get my things and get out. They ran us out because we believe in the Word of God. We don't believe in participating in the religious parties and fiestas, and we hold to what the Word of God says. They ran us out of town." Julia and her family believe that participating in these religious events would be counter to living a godly life as taught in the Bible.

While Sebastian and Julia are concerned about their family's future, they are delighted that the family's faith has grown and that they will continue to trust the Lord. "I am very firm in my faith," Julia stated, "and I know Jesus saved me and that He will continue. Our God is great, and I'm peaceful and trusting Him."

Their daughter, also named Julia, is a mother of two small children. Her husband abandoned the family, and she lost her job as a result of being expelled from the community. In addition, she said she was physically threatened by the political representative there. "He said that if he saw my face here in San Cristobal I would be sorry," Julia told us. "I felt very bad because we met all the obligations that were asked of us—the community service, we paid the fees—and we did nothing wrong. We are hoping for justice in the community and from state authorities."

Like her parents, Julia said that, rather than causing her to abandon her faith in Jesus, this persecution has had the opposite effect. She told me, "This experience has made me stronger, and I know I can trust God for the future." However, that does not mean she is without apprehension about her family. She went on to say, "I am concerned about my children because as they grow up as Christians, this will always be the way that it is; they will have to face the same things."

Julia's brother, Sebastian Jr., spent some time working in the United States. He has not regretted returning home to Mexico, even though he has faced many problems. He refuses to walk away from his faith in Jesus Christ or become bitter toward those who inflicted so much hardship on his family by evicting them from their village. Relatives and those he once considered friends will no longer have anything to do with them because of their decision to follow Christ, and that has been extremely painful. "I'm not angry with them," he explained. "I have prayed for them and asked the Lord to forgive them for what they did because they don't really understand what they are doing."

Sebastian Jr., who is firmly rooted in his relationship with Jesus Christ, admitted that he is concerned about the future. "But I know the value of my faith is in the Lord," he added. "It's the Lord who is going to give me the strength to keep going and help me in the future. When people hear what has

*Sebastian Jr.*

happened to us, then they will be praying for us. That will encourage us, and we will be able to accomplish what we need to."

Rachel and the Hernandez family are just a few of the millions of believers over the centuries who have suffered loss for their decision to put Jesus ahead of their families, friends, and communities. While the decision is right, it is never easy. Still, remember that it was not easy for Jesus to be separated from the Father in glory to come down here to a sinful world. He knows the pain involved in being pulled away from those you love and care about.

Many of the people I have interviewed over the years who have had to choose Jesus over family have also had the incredible blessing of realizing that they have a huge spiritual family all over the world! They have come to experience the truth of Jesus' promise: "And everyone who has left houses or brothers or sisters or father or mother or wife or children or lands, for My name's sake, shall receive a hundredfold, and inherit eternal life" (Matthew 19:29).

## OUR CHALLENGE: LOVING DESPITE REJECTION

Think of people in your local church family. Do you know some of their stories? How many of them have been rejected by their families for following God? Some have been ostracized because of poor choices in their past and have never been able to reconcile, even after they have come to Christ. Others have been forced out of their home countries and have left all that they own to be able to worship Christ freely.

It is one thing to think about people who have lost everything to follow Christ, and we cannot neglect to remember them in prayer. But it is another thing to be Christ's representative to people sitting in the pew next to us. You do not need to be everybody's best friend, but have you taken the time to listen to people's stories to find out how you can show them God's love?

As Christians, we love and honour our families, and there are entire ministries devoted to strengthening this basic institution planned and created by God. Yet God must come first in our affections; it was Jesus who said these hard words: "He who loves father or mother more than Me is not worthy of Me. And he who loves son or daughter more than Me is not worthy of Me" (Matthew 10:37). Our first loyalty is to our Lord, but sometimes, as the stories in this chapter reveal, serving and loving Jesus can create division within our families. However, that does not mean we will ever stop loving those who reject us because of our decision to have a relationship with God.

## CONSIDER & SHARE

- Are there ways in which you have become estranged from family members because of your relationship with Jesus? How does your family support and encourage you in your faith? Consider sharing this part of your journey with someone.

- When was the last time you invited a stranger over to show hospitality? (See Hebrews 13:2.) Who could you extend an invitation to this week? Perhaps begin by asking a widow or single person to join your family for a meal or event.

- Think of the many people who face conflict or rejection from their families for following Christ. Remember to pray for Christians who are being persecuted by their families today.

# CHAPTER 7

# REMEMBERING THOSE IN PRISON

*"Remember the prisoners as if chained
with them—those who are mistreated—since
you yourselves are in the body also."*
HEBREWS 13:3

Being put in prison because of a decision to follow Christ
has been going on for the past two thousand years. Many
of the believers in the early church—including some of the disciples—had their freedom taken away because they determined to be faithful to the gospel even when it conflicted with
the laws of the land or local religious leaders (see Acts 5:29).
Some, like Peter, were miraculously rescued; others, like John
the Baptist, were killed or died in prison.

For Christians in North Korea, their faith in Christ can cost
them their lives or their liberty. It is considered treason to worship anything outside of the ruling Kim family, who are pre-
sented as deity, or to follow any religion other than the cult
they founded, called Juche. As a result, many Christians are
arrested as traitors for worshiping God, and have been put to
death or sent to inhumane labour camps. Over the years, VOM
has received many reports of our brothers and sisters being
executed. Their crime is that they embraced the God of heaven

and stopped following the Juche cult. The following is just one example from North Korea, the Hermit Kingdom.

When authorities raided a religious meeting where twenty-three Christians had gathered, they arrested all of them. The three leaders of this group were given a quick trial, found guilty of treason, and executed. The other twenty were sent to a labour camp. Some of those who were leading the meeting that day had learned about Jesus and His offer of salvation while conducting business in China. Upon their return to North Korea they couldn't keep the Good News to themselves and boldly shared what they had learned about Christ's forgiveness—which is prohibited by the law. Those executed are now rejoicing in the presence of the Lord, and their struggle in this world is over. However, those in the labour camps are presently suffering along with thousands of other North Korean Christians who are paying a huge price to be identified with the Son of God.

We are told in Scripture that we are to remember believers who are in prison (Colossians 4:18). On this topic, the words of the author of Hebrews are very straightforward: "Remember the prisoners as if chained with them" (Hebrews 13:3). The word "remember" used in this passage means to be mindful of—to keep in mind. It is not used in a passive sense, but is meant to be engaging and active. Remembering our brothers and sisters in Christ is not something we should just think about and dismiss. To "remember" them requires action: we need to pray for them and to advocate for them. It might mean writing a letter to an embassy or the government of the country where these Christians are imprisoned, or providing support for their families.

When we participate in the Lord's Supper, we remember what Jesus did on the cross (see 1 Corinthians 11:24,25). It is not just giving mental assent to what our Lord did, but also being reminded of and contemplating His death on our behalf. In the same way, we actively remember our brothers and sisters who are locked up for their love for Jesus.

## Remembering Those in Eritrea

At the time of writing, an estimated three thousand Christians are imprisoned in shipping containers and military prisons in the East African nation of Eritrea. I think about their suffering and the pain of being separated from their families. I do not think about them in a passive way; I try to put myself in their place and empathize with what they and their families might be thinking or feeling. For example, several of the Christian leaders I had met in Eritrea were arrested a few months after we

*Shipping container prisons in Eritrea*

had visited and have now been languishing in terrible conditions since 2003.

Previously, there was general freedom to practice religion in Eritrea, but in 2002 the government announced it would recognize only four religious communities: the Orthodox Church of Eritrea, Sunni Islam, the Roman Catholic Church, and the Lutheran-affiliated Evangelical Church of Eritrea. Since then, thousands of evangelical Christians have been arrested for practicing what officials are calling "a new religion."

These followers of Christ live in deplorable conditions and endure torture at the hands of authorities. Many believers are held in metal shipping containers with no ventilation or toilet facilities, where daytime temperatures can soar above 40 degrees Celsius (over 100 degrees Fahrenheit).

Helen Berhane, a well-known gospel singer and member of the Rema Evangelical Church in Asmara, was arrested in May 2004, after she refused to sign a statement renouncing her Christian faith. While she was detained, she spent most of her time locked inside a metal shipping container with very little contact with her family, including her young daughter, or legal representation. She was also severely beaten and was denied access to proper medical care. In October 2006, she was released, most likely because of the international attention her imprisonment was attracting. Helen and her daughter, Eva, eventually escaped the country, and after eleven months in refugee camps in Sudan she and Eva were granted asylum in Denmark. However, due to the mistreatment Helen suffered while imprisoned, her legs were badly injured causing her to have trouble walking.

Even children are not exempt from persecution in Eritrea. In August 2008, authorities at the Sawa Defence Training Centre (a required military camp) burned hundreds of Bibles that had been confiscated from new students. When eight Christian students objected, they were locked up in metal shipping containers.

*Helen Berhane*

Despite this open persecution, the government continues to stand behind its official statement issued in May 2003 claiming that "no groups or persons are persecuted in Eritrea for their beliefs or religion." Evangelical leaders explain that the reason for their persecution is the Eritrean government's inaccurate perception of who these evangelicals are.

The government accuses the evangelical church of not being willing to defend the country, and therefore of causing division in the country by undermining unity. The Christian leaders say this is not true; they are very patriotic. Believers are also perceived as spies for the Ethiopian government, the CIA, and other Western intelligence services, and are falsely accused of transmitting AIDS throughout the country by being sexually immoral. All of this is propaganda from the Eritrean government in an effort to smear the evangelical Christians. The government considers Christians to be lazy people who waste their time in prayer and worship, and lumps evangelicals with Islamic fundamentalists as being dangerous to the country.

"Letay" grew up in an Orthodox family and came to know Jesus in 2000 through a revival that was sweeping through Orthodox churches in Eritrea. Her compassion for imprisoned Christians landed her in prison as well. Letay was a nurse at a military prison in the desert city of Assab. When she saw how her Christian brothers were suffering in prison because of their faith in Jesus, she and another Christian nurse were moved to help. "We tried to support these brothers by getting them money and clothing and some food," Letay explained. "But when we sent them some money later on, the security forces found the money and arrested my friend. She was interrogated, and finally, she spoke about me. We were arrested together because of that money."

As a result, Letay spent the next six months in a hot and stuffy prison. She said, "Prison is not easy; it was very difficult because they interrogated me and were saying a lot of bad words. I was afraid at first, and they separated me from everybody in a very small room. But later on they sent me to a bigger room with five other women, and we had a good time. We had plenty of time to pray and encourage each other." Letay went on to say, "There were two ladies who were there in the prison for different reasons. We shared the gospel with them, and they accepted Jesus Christ and we taught them to follow Him."

As a result of her time in prison, Letay is no longer afraid of what might happen to her. She was warned when she was released to stop reading the Bible and meeting with other evangelicals. Letay said she understands that she should submit to the government of Eritrea, regardless of how misguided it is, but her allegiance to Jesus comes first. "I know I have to obey the authorities as I read in the Bible," she said, "but there is a limit since this concerns my faith. I have to follow Jesus Christ and to have fellowship with my Christian brothers and sisters."

Letay knows she could end up in trouble with authorities again, but she is more concerned about those still in prison. She said, "I feel like I left my brothers and sisters there. It is very hard for me; I still have a burden for them." Letay has a deep understanding of what it means to remember those in prison. Can we do the same for our brothers and sisters in Eritrea and other nations around the world?

## Praying for Christians in Indonesia

"Andi" is an evangelist who leads almost eighty home cell groups in Indonesia. Each of these groups has six or seven believers from Muslim backgrounds as well as others interested in Christianity. He has found it effective to first use the Qur'an to teach about Jesus. "In the Qur'an, it states that the Bible is the light," he explained, "and through that statement I direct the students to read and study the Bible."

Andi's ministry is risky, difficult, and dangerous. At the time of our visit, he had already been arrested four times. Authorities have also brought him in for questioning after one of the young men he was working with gave officials his name. Police hauled Andi to the village headquarters and questioned him with several mullahs (Islamic clerics who have authority in the community). They asked why he was teaching about Jesus Christ in the area, who was funding his ministry, and if the money was coming from outside of Indonesia. Andi said it was a very intense grilling: "They started to ask which church was supporting me. I told them none of the churches or Christians were supporting me. I was just following what Jesus said to me. They asked me how many people there were like me doing the same thing. I said there were many people all over Indonesia.

The interrogators, the mullahs, the police, and the soldiers were confused."

He was interrogated and tortured for twelve hours. Another mullah intervened, and convinced police to release Andi into his custody. Officials thought the mullah was helping them, but it turned out that he was actually a secret believer!

Andi was not the only Christian who faced persecution. His students who had tried to keep their faith in Christ a secret were persecuted, too. "When the local Muslims found out my students had Bibles in their homes, they were very angry," he said. "They vandalized their houses and their small businesses. They destroyed their farmland." Yet rather than causing the students to become fearful, their persecution had the opposite effect: forty-seven of these new Christians boldly and publicly declared their faith in Jesus Christ by being baptized.

*"Andi"*

Andi knows that every Christian must "always be ready to give a defence" about the reason for their hope (see 1 Peter 3:15), so he made sure they were properly prepared. "I taught my students how to answer questions from the police when asked about their activities," he explained. "When they are asked, 'Why do you believe in Jesus Christ?' they say, 'Because in the Qur'an it says to believe in Jesus; even Mohammad said to believe in Jesus Christ.'"

Even though there is supposedly freedom of religion in Indonesia, to teach or even suggest that Jesus is greater than the prophet Muhammad of Islam is to risk great opposition and danger from militant Muslims. In daring to practice his religion, Andi has faced additional arrests: for handing out gospel tracts, for baptizing a former Muslim, and for sharing Scriptures with Muslims in a mosque. His longest incarceration lasted two years.

"In the beginning, I didn't realize the cost of following Jesus would include being put in jail," Andi shared. "My cell was near the bathroom, the smell was terrible and it was hard to sleep. The worst was the food. The guard didn't wash the plate; he just took someone else's plate and gave it to me. Sometimes the food was on the ground, dirty, and they gave it to me."

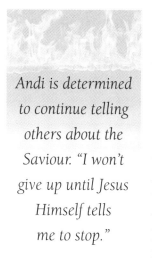

*Andi is determined to continue telling others about the Saviour. "I won't give up until Jesus Himself tells me to stop."*

For being a faithful witness and introducing many Muslims to Christ, Andi has been beaten while in prison. "It was unusual for someone to convince Muslims to become Christians," he said. "The guards were furious. Sometimes they urinated on my bed."

Andi has a wife and two small children and knows his ministry has greatly affected them, especially when he was put in prison. "My wife is always afraid about what I am doing, and my daughter asks me when I leave the house if she will see her daddy again. One of my children said, 'Daddy don't do those activities again.'" Despite the difficulties, and the risks for his family, Andi is determined to continue telling others about the Saviour. "I won't give up until Jesus Himself tells me to stop."

## The Faithful of Vietnam

Three tribal women from the Communist country of Vietnam traveled two days from their mountain village to meet with our team in Ho Chi Minh City (Saigon) to tell us their stories. Their husbands were prisoners—convicted for their conviction about following Christ. The persecution of Christians is much more prevalent in the rural areas of Vietnam, which is why these women came to us rather than our team going to their villages. It was felt our presence in their village would draw too much attention to the believers and could get them into trouble with the local authorities who oppose Christianity.

"Grace" told us that her husband was put in prison because he requested the freedom to follow his Christian faith and to reclaim land that had been taken away from him. Her husband was not alone: on April 10, 2004, a group of villagers protested the government's crackdown on their churches and illegal confiscation of properties.

Grace said her husband was sentenced to nine years and had served seven at the time she met with us. Her visits to him were limited to once or twice a year. For her, it is a sentence as well. "He's not at home. There is no one to do heavy labour at home, only women and children," she said. "We are afraid that the government will bring more difficulties upon our lives."

*"Grace," "Ruth," and "Deborah"*

"Ruth" has had a heavy burden as well. Her husband was sent to prison for twelve years. She suffers from hepatitis, has little support for her and her children, and was very emotional as she spoke of her ordeal. "We don't even have a bed; we just sleep on the floor. We don't have money to help the children get to school. They have to walk very far. We don't have a bike to travel long distances," Ruth explained.

"Deborah" said that she, Ruth, and Grace are discriminated against not only because their husbands are in prison, but also because of their faith. "The Christians are discriminated against; if you are Christian, you are not allowed anything."

In spite of these challenges, one thing these women have not lost is their faith—neither have their husbands. Deborah added that the Christians are considered political prisoners, so they are kept together away from the other inmates. However, that allows them to meet together. Like their husbands, these women also find comfort in meeting together and bringing their shared sorrow to God. They said that they pray for strength to stand and be faithful, and they hope others will pray for them.

Deborah, grateful for our visit and brief time of fellowship, told us, "I thank the Lord for bringing you from outside to come and knowing that we are in trouble. We ask you to continue to pray for us." Deborah's prayer was answered—her husband was released from prison a few months after our visit with her!

## OUR CHALLENGE: REMEMBERING OUR PERSECUTED FAMILY

As I mentioned earlier, the founder of The Voice of the Martyrs, Richard Wurmbrand, spent fourteen years in Romanian prisons because of his faith in Jesus Christ. Three of those years were spent in solitary confinement. Because of his commitment to Jesus, he knew something about being locked away. Pastor Wurmbrand wrote, "As for us, our hearts go out to the martyrs. Not that we pity them. Their chains are of pure gold. Their cross is perfumed. All those whose spiritual senses are alive know it. To Christians, prison has always been a delectable orchard where the sweetest nectar flows."

We need to remember those who are suffering in prisons, in shipping containers, and in places where their freedom has been taken away simply because they are followers of Jesus Christ. We are chained with them (Hebrews 13:3), but they also share in our freedom—a freedom we cannot afford to take for granted. Paul tells us, while sitting in chains in prison, that "the word of God is not chained" (2 Timothy 2:9). I have met many believers, who are not free to share the gospel themselves, who are encouraged to know that God's Word is still getting out. In the West we currently have that freedom. The question is: are we taking advantage of the freedom we have to talk about Christ openly?

## CONSIDER & SHARE

- If you were on trial for being a Christian, would there be enough evidence to convict you? (Don't count church attendance or church activities, as anyone can do them.) See James 2:18. How do you intentionally demonstrate your faith by what you do—that is different from good deeds done by those who don't know Christ?

- If you were imprisoned for your faith in Christ, how would you want people to "remember" you? Look for ways this week that you can actively remember—and take action to help—your brothers and sisters suffering in prisons worldwide.

- Pray God's blessing over those in prison today. Read 2 Corinthians 1:20. Take promises of Scripture (regarding peace, provision, forgiveness, etc.) and agree with God that they are as much for persecuted believers as they are for your family.

# CHAPTER 8

# GO AND MAKE DISCIPLES

*"And Jesus came and spoke to them, saying,
'All authority has been given to Me in heaven and on
earth. Go therefore and make disciples of all the nations,
baptizing them in the name of the Father and of the Son
and of the Holy Spirit, teaching them to observe all
things that I have commanded you; and lo, I am
with you always, even to the end of the age.'"*
MATTHEW 28:18–20

My wife and I intentionally disciple others, and we often use a relaxed and informal approach. Discipleship can take place over coffee as we share our lives with others, as well as in a group studying the Bible. When we meet with fellow believers, we like to encourage them and pray with them. We want to create an environment where others feel free to ask questions because this helps them to dig deeper into Scripture and grow in biblical knowledge. It is certainly not that we have all the answers; we are well aware that we are disciples as well. Rather, we are simply trying to be obedient to the Great Commission, in which Jesus commands all believers to be involved in making disciples.

Around the world, people embrace the cross of Jesus and receive His forgiveness. All who believe in Christ and choose to follow Him become His disciples. That is the very essence of being a Christian. However, producing disciples no longer seems to be the top priority for many churches in the Western world. Yes, there are fine churches all across the West committed to making disciples, but I have seen many people firsthand who call themselves followers of Jesus yet know very little of what the Bible teaches. These people really do not seem to be all that interested in studying Scripture and living a godly life. This is tragic and spiritually dangerous.

During one of several trips to Ethiopia, I met a number of young men who had amazing testimonies of how they came to faith in Jesus. I will share some of their stories, but what was even more impressive about them was their hunger for the Word of God and their desire to be both hearers and doers of the Word, as the Bible commands (see Matthew 7:21; James 1:22). Biblical illiteracy may be a problem where we live, but in many parts of the world, getting to know God through the Bible is at the top of the list. This is thanks in part to Christians who took our Lord's words literally when He said, "Go and make disciples."

## Ethiopia: Discipleship Is Not an Option

In the East African nation of Ethiopia, the gospel is spreading because of faithful and courageous Christians who are risking

*"Belay"*

everything to bring people to Jesus. Many of these new Christians have amazing stories to tell about how they were drawn to Christ as well as about the price they are willing to pay to follow Him. Why? Because they have been taught, and they know what is required of them as disciples of the Son of God.

Militant Muslims in southwest Ethiopia are destroying church buildings and violently attacking evangelical Christians. They not only want to stop the spread of Christianity, they also want to drive all Christians out of the country. Christian leader and evangelist "Belay" knows the dangers of being actively involved in proclaiming the gospel in this hostile area. He goes from village to village telling people that Jesus is the only way to heaven. Belay, who became a follower of Jesus out of an Orthodox background in 1991, has been insulted, beaten, arrested twice, and has had stones thrown at him. "They attempted to kill me four times, hoping that they will get me," Belay told me. "They killed another person because the Lord had told me to change my direction where I was heading."

His family has also felt the wrath of militant Muslims. Their home has been vandalized four times, and his children have been beaten when they leave the house. "They even tried to poison my children, but the Lord intervened and they didn't die," Belay added. "My family is suffering with me. Regardless of all these pressures, we continue to minister and work for the Lord."

Belay is targeted by the militant Muslims because he faithfully disciples, trains, and sends out missionaries and evangelists. Many of these young men have stayed in his house and he helps support them. He said, "They know that I'm the key person who is doing these things behind the scene, so they are targeting me." The enemies of the gospel realize that those who are serious about raising up true followers of Christ are the most dangerous to their cause.

One of the evangelists Belay has trained and discipled is "Ghebre." When I met up with Ghebre, he had led more than six hundred people to Christ over a three-year period in an area where mosques litter the landscape. Many of these new Christians are from Muslim backgrounds. He baptized sixty-five of them and started a church in his home. Ghebre goes from house to house telling people about Jesus and has been met with much opposition. On one occasion, he told me, hundreds of angry Muslims showed up at his house to kill him after Muslim leaders issued a death sentence on him. "They declared a *jihad*, a war on me, and whoever kills me will receive 80,000 Ethiopian *birr*. So in order to fulfill this declaration, five hundred people came to my house."

*"Ghebre"*

Ghebre was able to evade the mob that day but the death sentence remains. He has had several more threats against his life. His house was burned down and his personal belongings destroyed in the fire. With great conviction, Ghebre told me that he will not back down in his witness for Jesus. "I don't have any fear because it's not a man who called me; it's Jesus who called me to this ministry. Regardless of these dangers facing me, even last week I was witnessing about Christ from house to house in an area far away. All people on this earth, one way or another, will die. Nobody is going to live forever here. So dying for Jesus' sake is the glory. It's special; it's not like any ordinary death."

Among those Ghebre led to the Lord and discipled is "Hakim," a former Muslim. Hakim came to Christ after having a dream in which the Lord spoke to him. "I was very sick with a fever, malaria. I was not even able to speak. In the dream Ghebre was telling me about Christ, and he told me that if I became a Christian then I will be healed, but I refused. Then one night while I was sleeping, I had another dream. I saw

Ghebre coming to me, and he said, 'Unless you repent and become a Christian you will die with this sickness, but if you become a Christian you will be completely healed.' The following morning I made the decision to follow Christ." Hakim

*"Hakim"*

immediately went to Ghebre and told him about the dream. Ghebre prayed for Hakim, and he was healed from malaria! After such a dramatic and life-changing event, Hakim was hungry for the Word, and Ghebre was there to make sure he became a faithful follower of Christ.

Eighteen-year-old "Ibrahim" was a devoted Muslim, from a family of twelve generations of Muslims, so when Ghebre approached him to share the gospel Ibrahim was deeply offended and angry. He planned to kill Ghebre for telling him about Jesus. However, the Lord got hold of his heart and instead of seeking out Ghebre to murder him, Ibrahim asked questions about Jesus and not long afterward made a decision to follow Christ.

When Ibrahim's family learned he had become a Christian, they chased him away. With nowhere else to go, he slept in a tree at first, but would eventually go to live with some other young Christian men. Ibrahim was also discipled by Ghebre, and now he too is facing death threats from Muslims who heard about his conversion. He said it is hard to face these problems, but his newfound faith keeps him strong.

"Mohammad" faced persecution almost immediately after becoming a Christian at the age of eighteen. Following his conversion to Christ, a mob of three hundred people, including his family, took him away to be tortured. For three days, he was beaten and denied food, but he refused to return to Islam. The head of the local government threatened to kill him. As a result, Mohammad could not return home but said that will not stop him from preaching the Good News. If he had not understood that suffering for Christ would likely occur, Mohammad may very well have abandoned the Lord and returned to Islam, but he did not. He had been taught that "all who desire to live godly in Christ Jesus will suffer persecution" (2 Timothy 3:12).

Ghebre said he had made sure those he has led to the Lord, like Hakim, Ibrahim, and Mohammad, understand the cost and trials they would face as followers of Jesus. "I teach them about the gospel and the Word of God. I say, 'People who are persecuting you will come to know the Lord. So don't give up and return to your way of life.' They are willing to sacrifice with me, and die with me."

## North Korea: Bringing Light in the Darkness

North Korean Christians have endured much hardship, suffering, and often separation from family and friends. They have experienced despair and hopelessness after living under an oppressive and reclusive regime that rules with an iron fist and considers Christians enemies of the state. To the government, one of the worst offences is to become a Christian and worship Christ rather than the Kim family. Those who escape from the country and are caught are brought back and are often imprisoned in concentration camps, tortured, or killed.

"Tae" escaped in 1985 from North Korea because he heard there was freedom in China and South Korea. He was returned to North Korea by Chinese authorities and put in prison. As he was now considered a traitor, the North Korean authorities forced his wife to divorce him. He not only lost his wife, he lost his identity as a citizen of North Korea. "I was considered to have rejected my country and my parents after I left North Korea," Tae said. "I was not considered a human and was called by a number in prison."

While he was in China, Tae had heard the gospel from an elderly lady and had seen a Bible. Now sitting in prison, desperate, he decided to trust his life to Jesus Christ in 1987.

*"Tae" and "Shin"*

Following his release, Tae thought it was too dangerous to take his three young children with him when he escaped from North Korea a second time in 1996. It was a painful decision to leave them behind, but he felt he had no choice. He returned to China, and this time was able to avoid detection by the Chinese authorities. It would take five years before he could finally make his way to South Korea in 2001. Today he continues to pray not only for his family, but also for all North Koreans in the Hermit Kingdom. He has a strong desire to bring the life-changing message of the gospel to them. That is why he came to Underground University (UU), a ministry of Seoul USA, VOM's sister mission in Korea.

"I believe God has a plan for North Korean defectors who came to South Korea. It's important to do missionary work, send food, and do humanitarian acts in North Korea," explained Tae, "but it's also important to prepare North Korean defectors to be trained and equipped in the gospel to go back there. It's also important to pray for our families in North Korea."

In 2004 Tae married "Shin." A widow who had also lost her only daughter, Shin decided to leave North Korea for China in September 2003. "In the place I went, there were Christians and they shared about God. It was the first time I heard about God and the Bible, and I didn't understand at first," Shin told me. The believers would soon help her understand she needed to surrender her life to Jesus as her Saviour. "They were very friendly, and I could feel the love, so I opened my heart to Christ."

Shin adds that the North Korean government tried to keep its citizens blind to the outside world. "They shut our eyes and ears to see or hear," she said. "Whenever someone goes to a country like China and accepts Christ, when they come back and the authorities find out about that, they will send them to prison or kill them. It's not free for us to hear."

At first, Shin did not want Tae to have anything to do with ministry to North Koreans; she thought it was just too dangerous. "I didn't want him to get hurt or into trouble, but since we got married he continued his ministry to the North Korean people in China and South Korea. And as people came to Christ, I was touched by his ministry and his behaviour. Now I agree with his ministry, and that's why I joined UU." Tae and Shin know the dangers of ministry in North Korea and are fully aware that many have been killed for their faith in Christ.

Shin credited UU with helping her understand the cost of following Christ and being His disciple. "Through UU, I learned about people who have died for Christ and the martyr's life. I do have fears. It is not easy for me to dedicate my life to Christ," Shin admitted, but added, "I am willing to take the chance and go to North Korea to spread the gospel and take the consequences."

Tae said the teaching at UU about Christian martyrs, past and present, prepared him to give his life if necessary. "It's not that I would enjoy dying, but I will deal with it when the time comes."

The one-year curriculum includes *In the Shadow of the Cross*, written by Glenn Penner, former CEO of The Voice of the Martyrs Canada. Penner's book focuses on the biblical theology of persecution and discipleship. The curriculum also includes practical courses that take students into the mountains of

South Korea to develop team building, conflict resolution, and leadership skills.

Tae said that there he learned about teamwork—a key to being a follower of Christ. "I have team members. Throughout the training, I thought about Jesus Christ and how we are the Body of Christ. We have to function together. If we don't work together, we would be handicapped and wouldn't be one body. This training helped me to cooperate with others."

Although Shin was told by her doctor that she should not walk long distances because of a bad back, she was able to meet the physical demands of the outing with the help she received from fellow students as well as strength from the Lord. "I felt the teamwork was great. I didn't expect to get help from the others. I appreciate the help I got from my brothers and sisters during the training," she said.

Although North Korea is one of the most closed countries in the world to the gospel, the Lord is drawing North Koreans to Himself and is using students at Underground University as instruments to proclaim the message of forgiveness, freedom, and hope in Jesus Christ—the same message that brought them true freedom. They are disciples making disciples as they follow the instructions of the Great Commission.

## Making Disciples in Indonesia

In 2005, "Ishmael's" life was falling apart in Indonesia. He had many addictions. His wife, Faiza, was ready to leave him and take their two children with her. "When Ishmael was working in the bus terminal," said Faiza, "he always had problems with some things. He was a drunkard and liked to play with prostitutes."

Ishmael does not deny what he had become. "I worked in the terminal and the life there was very hard. Many of us drivers were drunks. We went to prostitutes and gambled," he admitted.

Ishmael said that despite a life full of sin, he was a devout Muslim, even going from mosque to mosque to teach the

Qur'an. "I was in a Muslim fundamentalist group. In December 2005, I was ordered to stop the Christmas service led by Pastor Ibrahim." But instead of interrupting the service as planned, Ishmael listened to Pastor Ibrahim speak and later approached him to find out more about Jesus.

"As I prayed for Ishmael, he began crying," the pastor explained. "He had come to the meeting checking up on Christians and what we were doing in that building. But after hearing about Jesus in the meeting, he wanted to know more."

Ishmael said that as Pastor Ibrahim prayed for him, something amazing happened. "I felt something new in my heart. The pastor gave me a Bible and a Qur'an and he told me to think about my life." For the next six months, Ishmael did a comparison between the Bible and the Qur'an. "Pastor Ibrahim helped me to understand more. After six months, I finally decided to become a Christian."

Faiza was stunned by the transformation in Ishmael's life. "When I saw the dramatic change in my husband, from that moment I became interested in Christianity. I wanted to know how my husband could be changed so much," she said. "We became Christians."

Within a month of turning both their lives over to Jesus, they were baptized and learned to be disciples under the instruction of Pastor Ibrahim. Ishmael and Faiza also began to encounter persecution from their family members. "We faced many challenges from the Muslim community. We were expelled from our village after we came to Christ. Even my family drove us out of our village. We were disowned by our families," Faiza said, adding that it was very difficult. "But I have a strong faith in the Lord and never want to withdraw from the Lord."

After being threatened by the militant Muslims and forced from their village, Ishmael and Faiza relocated to another area where they own a house. They live, at least for now, at peace with their neighbours—many of whom are Muslims. "When we faced these problems," Ishmael told me, "I had learned from the Bible that the Lord is full of compassion and that I must stand on the truth of the Bible and follow what it teaches. I must be patient and not take revenge."

Ishmael has been involved in full-time ministry since 2006, just one year after becoming a follower of Jesus. He was taught right from the beginning what was expected of him as a Christian. "I tell anyone I meet about Jesus," Ishmael explained. "I don't bring my Bible; I bring the Qur'an and show them that in the Qur'an, Jesus is well known on the earth in life after death. Nine hundred verses in the Qur'an tell about Jesus."

*"We were disowned by our families. But I have a strong faith in the Lord and never want to withdraw from the Lord."*

With the help of Pastor Ibrahim, Ishmael leads several house churches of Muslim converts including one in his own home. Faiza has been amazed at what God is doing through them. "I'm very happy, very joyful to see around thirty-five to forty believers every Friday come to this house and praise the Lord." Ishmael also travels up to four hours by motorcycle to disciple new believers from Muslim backgrounds.

Ishmael and Faiza have five children, a daughter-in-law, and one grandchild. If persecution does come again, Faiza knows that her family will stand firm. "If one day there are problems, I will never leave Jesus, because Jesus will never forsake me and my family."

Ishmael's mentor and friend Pastor Ibrahim is very effective in discipling new believers because of the many trials he has endured as a Christian in a Muslim country. He knows first-hand the importance of getting disciples grounded in the Bible and the cost of being committed to Jesus. Ibrahim has faced great hostility because of his ministry, with the most serious incident occurring in 2007. As he was leading a house church meeting with twenty people from Muslim backgrounds, a mob of several hundred militant Muslims showed up and threatened to kill them and burn down the house with them inside. Ibrahim said he tried to keep everyone calm. "I told the believers to move into the kitchen and keep the Bibles and Christian books in a safe place, while I stayed in the living room. The Muslims outside were yelling at us, saying, 'Let's get in the house and kill these Christians and cut their throats.'"

Pastor Ibrahim said the Muslims, some of whom were heavily intoxicated, started to vandalize the property and took gasoline from two motorbikes. "From inside we could smell the gasoline," Ibrahim said. "Some of the believers wanted to escape from the house, but were afraid because they could see the gasoline by the door."

*"I asked them if they wanted to follow Christ even after all these incidents and they said yes, they wanted salvation."*

The mob tried to set the house on fire but lost the matches in all the confusion. By then, soldiers from another village—along with local police and the village leader—had arrived at the house and tried to settle the issue. Eventually, the mob dispersed, and Ibrahim was delighted that this attack did not cause any of these young Christians to turn away from faith in Jesus. "When the incident happened, I was teaching new believers, as well as some who were still Muslims. I asked them if they wanted to follow Christ even after all these incidents and they said yes, they wanted salvation," he explained. "I told them that to follow Jesus has a price, and you must carry the cross of Christ."

Ibrahim, Faiza, and Ishmael, along with countless other faithful and brave followers of Jesus Christ, continue to devote their lives to helping others in Indonesia discover the freedom that can be found only in Jesus. They are taking seriously the

Savior's command to go and make disciples. This is not an option, but a matter of spiritual survival in a country hostile to the gospel.

## OUR CHALLENGE: PRIORITIZING DISCIPLESHIP

We may not face the same intensity of persecution in the West as our brothers and sisters in countries like Ethiopia, North Korea, and Indonesia, but many professed Christians in "free countries" are not only not actively making disciples, but they are not even being discipled themselves. Discipleship should be a top priority for every church in every country, and must be the lifestyle of everyone who claims to be a follower of Christ. We are told in the Bible to pass on what we have learned to those who will faithfully pass it on to others (2 Timothy 2:2). It is a matter of spiritual survival!

Over the years, I have seen many people I thought were Christians drift away from the faith. Why does this happen? There are many reasons, but often it is a lack of understanding of what the Bible teaches and not really knowing the cost of following Jesus. One reason, I believe, is misguided teaching from pulpits, Christian media, and books. Many today are emphasizing the wrong things. Rather than total surrender and complete devotion to Jesus, we are hearing about how to make our life easier and better. All too often, a Christianity without the cross and sacrifice is being taught, and the kind of "disciple" that teaching produces will not be able to withstand the attacks of the enemy and his forces. Let us take encouragement from our brothers and sisters who are paying a huge price to be passionate disciples of Jesus.

## CONSIDER & SHARE

- Who has been the greatest influence in your Christian walk? What do you appreciate about that person?

- Have you shared with others what has been entrusted to you? Are there Christians who are younger in the faith whom you could help to disciple? Ask God for guidance in approaching them while thinking through a plan to help them grow.

- We often appreciate qualities we see in others because we want others to see the same thing in us. What do you think people see in you? If there are ways in which you need to be a better example, what can you do to improve?

# CHAPTER 9

# LIVING FOR ETERNITY

*"In My Father's house are many mansions; if it were
not so, I would have told you. I go to prepare a place
for you. And if I go and prepare a place for you,
I will come again and receive you to Myself;
that where I am, there you may be also."*

JOHN 14:2,3

When I was five or six years old, I comprehended the concept of death, and it scared me that someday I would not be here anymore. Two or three years later, I was introduced to church and heard about God and the afterlife. While I have always believed in heaven, I did not understand how to get there until much later. Still, the seeds had been planted.

One afternoon when I was in my early twenties I was listening to the radio with my dad, and I heard on the news that someone I knew from high school had died in a car accident. Suddenly, he was gone. It was a pivotal point that caused me to think about heaven and what happens when you die. I started to ask the deep questions about life, and I had a conversation with my dad (who was not a Christian) about it.

I wondered, *If there is a heaven, how do I get there?* I also searched for answers to the question "What happens when you die?" from different religious groups. During my spiritual quest over the next year, I had a few Christians in my life, and as I asked them questions they pointed me to the truth. Over time I decided to do what they said—I put my trust in Jesus because I realized He was the only way to eternal life. I repented of my sins and began a relationship with Him that has intensified over the years, and I long to see Him face to face! I now have an eternal perspective and no longer believe as I once did that when life ends everything just fades to black. In fact, I have learned to live with the reality of suffering in this life, and it motivates me for the life that is to come.

For many Christians, the pain they have had to endure on this side of heaven will stay with them the rest of their lives on earth. While they love their families and friends in the here and now, they are living for another age—a better age. The things they have gone through have caused such heartache that looking beyond this life is what gives them the strength to get up each day and keep going. In this chapter, we will meet two ladies from different parts of the world who have suffered terribly but still want to make their lives count for God's kingdom. Why? Because they are living for eternity, an existence where all the pain and suffering from this life will be gone forever.

## Hajara: "Wipe Away All Tears"

In the early morning hours of February 22, 2000, Hajara Magaji suffered an unspeakable tragedy. Militant Muslims, upset that Christians were trying to block Shariah law in Kaduna State, Nigeria, went on a rampage. Hearing an angry mob approaching, about thirty family and friends ran to Hajara's home, as the Christians tried to decide what they could do to survive the attack. The mob soon surrounded the house where the believers had gathered.

Hajara recalled the tragic events of that day: "I heard my name being called from outside. They said they were going to kill me and my children. I asked, 'Why?' All they said was,

'Today we are going to kill you and your family.' They started throwing rocks at the house, and were throwing burning tires inside. Some were armed with guns. We were shouting for help. The men inside the house said we should get ready to fight back; we either live or die." According to Hajara, the women began gathering up the rocks that had

*Hajara Magaji*

been thrown at them so the men could try to defend themselves, even if it was a feeble attempt, while the children were praying. This went on from 7 a.m. until noon. Although the believers had been trying to put out the flames started by the burning tires, it eventually proved futile. Hajara said, "The mob shut off the water flow into our house, so we couldn't put out the fire. We were all very tired."

With the house burning, Hajara's seventeen-year-old son, Amos, stood up and took charge. "He was a quiet leader; he was a committed Christian," Hajara said. "He decided that today he will be the pastor and started exhorting those in the house to get their hearts right before they leave this world—we are likely to die. We were trying to fight back and pray to God. We all prayed. I was ready to depart the world; I didn't know if I would survive the battle. I saw some of my children on the ground dead; other people in the house were shot down."

Hajara's husband told her to do her best to rescue some of their children, but said things appeared to be hopeless. "There was no way to get out of the house. It was surrounded. He told me to still try. I attempted to escape with two children," she said.

115

Hajara's daughter, Sarah, then age ten, and six-year-old Benjamin fled the burning house with their mother. Hajara was stabbed and had rocks thrown at her, but despite her injuries she managed to escape. The attackers grabbed the two children, however, and they were taken to a Muslim neighbour's home where their captors tried to force them to convert to Islam. Benjamin said Sarah was not about to do that. "My sister said that since they have killed all our family, she cannot become a Muslim." A short time later, a Muslim neighbour of the family argued that these were just children, and convinced the captors to release Benjamin and Sarah.

That day in February 2000, Hajara lost her husband, four children, two grandchildren, and her daughter-in-law. "When I remember Job in the Bible, despite all he suffered, he trusted in God," Hajara told me. "He got what was lost restored to him. He was given beautiful daughters. I know I can't have children again, but pray for me and my children Sarah and Benjamin that God will bless these two children and cause His blessings to be on Sarah so she will have many children and be a comfort to me."

Although one of Benjamin's legs was badly burned during the attack, aside from scars he has no permanent injuries. He told me that he would one day like to be the president of Nigeria, so he can help others like himself who have lost parents or other loved ones due to violence against Christians.

*Benjamin Magaji*

As for his mother, Hajara said Isaiah 25:8 been a great comfort to her in the midst of such heartache. In this passage, the Lord promises to wipe away all tears and swallow up death forever. As Hajara shared that Scripture with us, tears were streaming down her face. She truly knows of what she speaks!

Hajara is living for another age, and that longing for eternity is giving her hope now. That same comfort of heaven, where all pain will be gone, is also what keeps "Yang" going.

## Yang: "So Much Heartache"

"Yang" is a North Korean exile now living in South Korea who has known much pain and suffering in her life, both physically and emotionally. Yang described life in North Korea as unbearable and brutal, and with food very scarce she and others would do whatever they could to survive. "I was living in the poorest village in North Korea," Yang told me. "We had to eat sand, which was hard to get. I had to go far away to get this sand, and only a few people got some. I also had to eat wood. It was difficult to go to the bathroom." Yang said ten or eleven people in her village were starving to death every day at the peak of the fam-

*"Yang"*

ine in the mid-1990s. Many were suffering mental breakdowns and enduring unspeakable horrors.

Like many followers of Christ, Yang found that her husband wanted nothing to do with her once she became a Christian. In 1998, Yang was desperate to help her family, which included two young daughters. She snuck into China to try to make some money, but with the Chinese police looking for North Korean defectors, she was unable to find work and returned home. After it was discovered that she had left, she was beaten by government authorities and viewed as a traitor.

117

Four years later, she again fled North Korea to China with the hope of earning some money. It was there Yang met an ethnic Korean woman who was operating a rice-selling business. This woman was a Christian who took seriously Paul's words to "pray without ceasing" (1 Thessalonians 5:17). "Before this lady left the house she prayed. At work she prayed," Yang said. "I asked her what she was doing, and she said she believed in God and went to church. I asked her what church was. She told me about the existence of God and said if I met God, I would be blessed." This bold believer explained how Yang could not only know about God, but could have a relationship with Him and be with Him forever!

Yang gave her life to Christ, then she returned to North Korea hoping to reunite with her children. Conditions had improved somewhat in the country, and while there was not an abundance of food, at least some was available. Yang began a business, now as a Christian. "I had a business selling noodles and rice in North Korea, and as I learned in China, I prayed when I was doing my business," explained Yang. "The lady working beside me asked what I was doing. I didn't say anything. Some of my relatives from China also saw me praying and told the lady I was a Christian, and she told the authorities."

The authorities brought Yang in for questioning, since being a Christian is seen as an act of treason in North Korea. They could not find any evidence that she had become a Christian, but that did not stop the authorities from beating and torturing her. Yang said this went on for a month. "They used a shovel to beat me. My body became blue everywhere. After I was released, I was followed everywhere by the authorities. My parents-in-law didn't even treat me like a human, so I decided to leave the country again."

Yang returned to China in 2003, and soon after arriving she was kidnapped by human traffickers and another nightmare began. She was sold into slavery as a maid, where she was repeatedly raped. "I was sold to a businessman who owned a department store and I was locked in the house. The telephone line was cut and the doors were locked from the outside, so I couldn't run away," Yang told me in tears. "I was a slave there for six weeks before I escaped."

Yang's troubles in China continued. She did not speak the language, and just trying to survive was extremely difficult. In the winter of 2006, along with a friend, she decided to try to make it to South Korea. With the help of some brokers, who for a fee help people get out of the country, Yang and her friend were brought close to the Mongolian border. They would have to travel the rest of the way on their own.

The Mongolian winters can be treacherously cold—twenty degrees below zero Celsius, or worse—and Yang was six months pregnant. She and her friend got lost wandering in the snow and could not find the guards at the border garrison for three days. In the extreme conditions, Yang had a miscarriage, then placed the baby in a handbag. "I didn't know what to do, but I had to walk. I hung the bag around my neck and walked all night," Yang said. "All around us were skeletons—bones of North Korean defectors who didn't make it. My friend started to rip my clothes because I didn't give her bread."

But Yang did not have any food; her friend was hallucinating. Devastated, Yang watched her friend die in the snow in the bitterly cold temperatures. She was very emotional as she recalled that horrible event. "Her heart finally stopped, but I will never forget her eyes—she was crying and looked at me. After my friend died, I think I was in shock. I fell asleep, and when I woke up, I felt warm; I thought it was sunshine," Yang told me. "I had one hand on my friend and one hand on my baby. It was still dark. I got up and prayed for the Lord to save me."

Two more days would pass before Yang was finally discovered by patrolling Mongolian border guards who found her lying in the snow. She was unable to open her eyes or move. Yang was taken to a hospital in Mongolia, the bodies of her friend and baby left behind.

Yang suffered severe frostbite in both of her feet. Little could be done by the medical staff in Mongolia, so she was flown to the South Korean Armed Forces Medical Command in Seoul. Yang's toes on her left foot were amputated because of the frostbite, and a nerve from her thigh was transplanted to her foot. There was also some damage to her right foot. Even though this happened in 2006, she is still in constant pain.

With all that Yang has been through, it is amazing that she has been able to persevere and look to the future. She credits her faith in Jesus Christ as the reason she has hope, but admits her faith has been tested. "When I almost died in Mongolia, I prayed for God's help. My baby died. My friend died. God didn't answer my prayers. At the time I was bitter," Yang admits. "But God gave me the heart to live, and I kept praying to live. He saved me. Now I will be a more devoted Christian and want to be a missionary for God. I am learning more about God, and I will live for Him."

*We need to live in such a way that we are reminded daily to "set our minds" on heaven where our Lord Jesus is seated.*

Yang told me she wants to minister to the people of North Korea and point them to the hope of heaven. "I want to make sure I spread the Word of God. I want people to know there is an invisible God who we are to believe in whether we are in North Korea, China, or anywhere in the world. I also want to tell the world about real life in North Korea, that there are people like me in North Korea. It's a country that doesn't believe in God. I choose to do missionary work because there are many North Korean defectors living in the world. I want them to know I survived, and I will be more persuasive for them to believe in Christ."

Like Hajara in Nigeria and believers all over the world, Yang looks forward to heaven, not only because she will be there someday, but also because it gives her a reason to live and have hope on this side of eternity. The pain will linger in her memory as long as she has breath, but what an incredible hope that someday that pain will be gone forever!

## OUR CHALLENGE: FOCUSING ON ETERNITY

Even though most of us have not faced the kinds of tragedy and evil that were committed against our sisters in this chapter, we too can focus on heaven. The apostle Paul had instructed the Colossian church to do the same, stating, "If then you were raised with Christ, seek those things which are above, where Christ is, sitting at the right hand of God. Set your mind on things above, not on things on the earth" (Colossians 3:1,2). Paul was doing effective kingdom work on earth because he really understood what it meant to be seated with Jesus in heaven.

One of the many lessons I have learned from our persecuted family is that they are living for another age. Our challenge is to do the same. But we need more than a mental acknowledgment of that truth; we need to live in such a way that we are reminded daily to "set our minds" on heaven where our Lord Jesus is seated. It will help us keep an eternal perspective and bring us hope and joy, causing us to live holy and godly lives while making us effective. (See Colossians 3:1–14.)

In my early days as a Christian, I remember hearing the expression that some believers were too heavenly minded to be any earthly good. I disagree with that. I now believe we need to be heavenly minded, in order to be any earthly good. Where is your focus?

## CONSIDER & SHARE

- "This world is as close to heaven as some people will experience. For Christians it is as close to hell as we will experience." What do you think of this saying? Does it motivate you? If so, how? Share your thoughts with someone today.

- Hajara found comfort in the promise of Isaiah 25:8. How does that verse encourage you in your times of difficulties?

- Read Philippians 3:20. How often do you think about heaven? Make it a discipline to consider it often.

# CHAPTER 10

# TAKE UP YOUR CROSS

*"Then He said to them all, 'If anyone desires
to come after Me, let him deny himself,
and take up his cross daily, and follow Me.'"*
LUKE 9:23

If you have been around the church for any length of time you've probably heard many references in sermons to "taking up your cross." What did Jesus mean by this radical statement? To better understand what was necessary to be a faithful follower, and to know the level of commitment He was requiring, we need to look at what He said just before and after this statement. The verse is sandwiched between Jesus telling His disciples that He would suffer many things, be killed, and be raised again (v. 22), and saying that whoever loses his life for His sake will save it (v. 24). Jesus was calling His disciples—all those who would follow Him throughout the centuries—to total devotion.

A question I often ask myself is, "Have I taken up my cross?" Taking up the cross means putting to death our fleshly nature, denying our selfish desires, and committing ourselves fully to the kingdom of God and its purposes. I often wrestle with wanting what is best for me and worrying about what I should get in return for my efforts, rather than wanting what is best for others and fulfilling God's purposes in my life. I know I should put others ahead of myself, but my flesh wants me to be satisfied. Denying ourselves is not what comes naturally to us, which is why we must take up the cross. To be sold-out followers of Jesus requires nothing less than death to self.

Many persecuted believers I have met have counted the cost and it is often very obvious that they have taken up their cross. However, taking up the cross will look different for every believer.

For me, taking up the cross has meant getting out of my comfort zone. While I enjoy traveling, I do not like being away from my wife and children for weeks at a time. I frequently become ill after eating food foreign to my system. Many of the places where we go to meet our persecuted family are in dangerous areas where outsiders can be targets for kidnapping or violence.

There are often extremes in weather when traveling from Canada in winter to the heart of Africa in summer. There is also an emotional toll from hearing hundreds of stories, seeing the individuals' tears, and feeling their misery. At times I have trouble sleeping. However, going without the comforts of home for a short period pales in comparison to the conditions of everyday life for many faithful believers around the world.

In this chapter, we are going to meet some Christian leaders from countries where torture, imprisonment, and death are all too common for those who follow Jesus. All of them have taken the words of Jesus seriously and have taken up their cross. They understand the words of Paul in Galatians 5:24 that "those who are Christ's have crucified the flesh with its passion and desires." Let's be challenged together as we meet these pastors and evangelists from Vietnam, Iran, and Colombia.

## Enduring Faith in Vietnam

"Kahn," a pastor from a village in northern Vietnam, was arrested because of his ministry activities and cruelly hung by his thumbs. "They took me to the police station and tortured me," Kahn told me, his voice choked with emotion. "They used something to tie my thumbs and one of my toes and hang me on the wall for three hours." While the pain was unbearable, his faith in God helped him to endure it. However, this would not be Kahn's last encounter with persecution.

Kahn faces additional risks as he travels to area villages to preach the gospel and meet with Christians to disciple them. He said, "I believe that Jesus can help me to get through this and help me to lead the church, and so I just keep praying. When I walk through the forest, through the jungle, I'm not afraid of tigers or scary animals, but I am afraid that the government

*Kahn: "They hung me by my thumbs!"*

will find out where I'm going." Kahn prayed he would find other believers who would help him train and disciple the people of his church. God heard his prayer, and he was able to connect with a network of believers in an underground Bible school who have the same desire to evangelize and disciple.

For fifteen years, Christianity was almost unheard of among his tribe, but today, the people in the tribal areas make up Vietnam's fastest-growing church. Let me introduce you to three other men in Vietnam who are as passionate as Kahn about spreading the gospel of Jesus Christ. All have taken up their cross and are willing to put their safety on the line. They are Tien, Minh, and Peter, from a mountain region in the north.

Tien first heard of Jesus through a radio program that was broadcast into Vietnam. Later, he witnessed how in a matter of one night, two villages of about seventy families gave up worshiping the ghost of their community (a type of ancestor worship). "I was very surprised," he said, "and I thought there must be a God, an amazing God that made that happen."

After deciding to become a Christian, Tien has faced several imprisonments for his Christian activity, but it has not deterred this young man from evangelism. When asked why, his answer was straightforward and clear: "Because the Bible says whoever follows God and carries the cross every day He will give life, and if you try to save your life it will be taken it away. So we follow Christ."

Following Christ has also meant much trouble for Minh. He practiced idol worship his whole life. But when he became seriously ill, he could not find relief. In his culture, those who were sick were often required to offer expensive sacrifices. "I had spent all my money to buy the sacrifice as required by the culture, but I ran out of money," Minh explained. "Normally it's a chicken. Then if there isn't a healing, a pig, then a cow. If there still isn't a healing, two cows and then three cows." As a result, people go deep into debt spending money on these sacrifices.

With nowhere else to turn, Minh then went to a Christian in the village who prayed for him. He was healed—not just physically, but spiritually, as he gave his life to Christ. Rejoicing that he had come to know the one true God, Minh publicly destroyed his idols. Many in his community were angered by this, and he was brutally beaten by the police.

Minh is not fighting back; instead, he is equipping himself to teach and preach the salvation he has found. He wants his persecutors to come to Christ as well. "Please pray for the evil people in the village," he pleaded, "so God will calm them down and help them to understand that He is powerful and loving, so they may know Him personally."

As these Vietnamese men have studied the Bible, they discovered that being persecuted for following Jesus is nothing new. Peter, another believer who has been arrested many times for preaching, takes this persecution in stride. "The government says there is freedom of religion, but actually there is a lot of persecution among Christians and other groups. But I always have freedom," Peter said boldly, "because it doesn't matter whether they allow us or not—I still do what I'm called to do."

During our meeting with these devoted Christians, one of our team members asked Peter why they are so persecuted while believers in much of the world are not. His answer was straight to the point: "I think one of the reasons people are not persecuted is because the church hasn't sent people out to evangelize and do something for God. The reason we are persecuted is because we are active and are sending people out to evangelize others and get people saved."

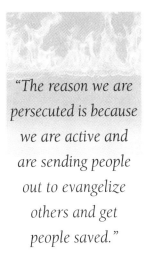

*"The reason we are persecuted is because we are active and are sending people out to evangelize others and get people saved."*

In any battle, the enemy fire is focused on those on the front-lines, those engaged in the battle who are encroaching on the enemy's territory. Any soldiers still sitting in the barracks, who pose no threat, are ignored and safe from attack. In our spiritual battle, are you doing anything to be in the enemy's crosshairs?

## Carrying the Cross in Iran and Iraq

Nader and Aram lead a house church in Iraqi Kurdistan and are also doing significant work among Kurdish refugees, especially those in the refugee camps. They are passionate about bringing the hope of Christ to those who are without hope, because Nader and Aram know what that situation is like.

Brothers who came from a Muslim family, Nader and Aram grew up in the unstable and volatile country of Iran. Their world as they knew it changed forever after Aram was involved in a car accident in 2000. He was badly injured and suffered severe head trauma. The nineteen-year-old said he had a near-death experience at the hospital, and at that moment he encountered God. "I felt peace; it was amazing, unbelievable peace," said Aram. Then I went back to my body and I saw the doctor and others around me as they tried to bring me back to life. They had things like the electric shock paddles, which they put on my chest to bring me back."

*Nader and Aram*

Aram said that is where his story with the God of heaven began. He had more dreams and visions and eventually gave his life to Jesus. He shared these experiences with his brother, and Nader also had a supernatural encounter with Jesus where the Lord spoke to him. Like his brother, he too decided to follow Christ.

By 2003, Nader and Aram were active in reaching Iranian Kurdish Muslims with the gospel, and their evangelism efforts caught the attention of government officials. The brothers were harassed and threatened in order to get them to stop their Christian activity. "Many young people came and joined our Bible study, and when the government officials found out about it they were trying to find the names of all those people through us." Aram and Nader were brought in for questioning but refused to give the names of these young people, mostly from Kurdish backgrounds, who were interested in finding out more about Christianity. Fearing for their safety, the brothers fled Iran and went to Iraqi Kurdistan.

Aram and Nader missed their family, but as their Christian faith deepened, so did their desire to serve Christ. After being baptized in 2004, the brothers and some others started a house church and were sharing the gospel with Kurdish Muslims—many of whom came from Iran. "When we tried to convert people, the Iranian government found out about us," Aram said. "They didn't like it, and they put a lot of pressure on our family to bring us back to Iran."

The Iranian government arrested their father and tried to force him to convince Aram and Nader to return to Iran. Their father refused and, as a result, he was tortured for more than a week. Nader was deeply distressed when he found out what happened. "It was a really hard time," he said. "We were under pressure and harassed and missing our family and our dad, but we also had happiness inside and we had God. He appeared and said, 'I am your heavenly Father.'"

Nader and Aram have been kidnapped three times and taken to the Iranian Consul in Iraq, where they were accused of being spies due to their Christian activity. On the first occasion, a government official from Iran threatened them. "He said, according to the Qur'an law and according to the law that has been made in the Iranian parliament, you should be executed and you should die because you changed your background and are like dirt on the earth and should be removed," Aram told me.

Nader's wife, Katreen, and her family are from Baghdad and were living with Nader and Aram and their widowed mother in Erbil, Kurdistan, when we visited with them. Katreen and her family have experienced firsthand the wrath of al-Qaeda. The Islamic terrorist organization bombed their church and many other church buildings in the Iraqi capital. "We have hope," Katreen shared, "but we have no future." She was expressing the uncertainty and despair shared by many Iraqi Christians. She knows their hope is eternity with Christ; but on this earth, the situation for Iraq looks grim.

Despite the threats and danger, Nader and Aram will continue to bring the gospel to the Kurds. Nader said the opposition they have encountered to the message of the cross has only strengthened their faith, and they know where that strength comes from. "I have a very powerful and strong person behind me," Nader declared, "and that person is Jesus Christ!"

## Rolo: Evangelist to the Guerrillas

Evangelist "Rolo" is one of the few who dare to enter the Marxist rebel–controlled areas of Colombia to bring the saving message of Jesus Christ to those living there. Rolo not only reaches out to the Revolutionary Armed Forces of Colombia (FARC) guerrillas, but he also brings encouragement to the pastors and villagers. These people are trapped by the FARC and prevented from leaving without permission. Rolo understands the situation very well—he used to be a guerrilla.

As a teenager, Rolo had gotten involved in the drug trade where he was introduced to the FARC. "We produced a lot of cocaine in some big camps run by the guerrillas," said Rolo, "and I took a liking to the guerrillas and decided to become one of them." From ages fourteen to twenty-nine, Rolo was devoted to the guerrilla movement because it promised to even out the wealth of the country. Believing the movement would fix the social and economic problems plaguing Colombia and better everyone's lives, he began to study Marxism, the ideology behind it. As a part of the FARC, his jobs included recruiting farmers and youth to join the guerrillas.

*"Rolo" with a FARC guerrilla*

In Rolo's mind, the goals of the movement justified the use of violence. "There was a lot of violence because we were defending our camps and the areas where we had control over the people," Rolo told me matter-of-factly. "Any strangers who came in who couldn't explain why they were there were killed. Anyone suspected of being a government spy was killed. There were a lot of these things going on all the time."

Even in the midst of all the terrible things he witnessed and participated in, Rolo had not forgotten about some Christians he had heard singing in the jungle when he was fifteen years old. The thoughts of a God he knew nothing about would come and go over the years, even though he claimed to be an atheist.

Eventually, the guerrilla movement decided to expel all the Christians in the area where Rolo was stationed. "As I was with the guerrilla movement, I was trying to change and make the world a better place. We supposedly had these lofty ideals," he explained, "but in actual practice, I saw that we were the ones committing the injustice toward the Christians. I began to see their testimony and example, and that made me realize that God is real—and I wanted to be on His side."

There was one Christian who did not leave when everyone else was forced to flee. Rolo asked him if the God he believed in was capable of helping him out of all his problems. When the man said yes, Rolo said yes to Jesus Christ and became one of His followers.

Not long afterward, Rolo's life was on the verge of ending. "After the guerrillas expelled the Christians, another armed group, a paramilitary group, came in and went after the guerrillas. They had a list of people who were with the guerrillas, and my name was on that list. They captured me and took me off to kill me," Rolo said. Fearful, the new believer called on the God he knew could help him: "I cried out to the Lord and said to Him, 'If You save me, I will serve You the rest of my life.'" Rolo's life was spared, and he has made good on his promise to serve the Lord.

"Soon after I prayed that prayer, instead of executing me, they let me go. When I got back to the jungle, I got beside a big tree and wept and prayed for about an hour. Later, the man who brought me to the Lord gave me his Bible; it was the only one he had." Rolo would constantly read and study God's Word. The more he read, the more he wanted to go back into the jungle and tell others about the life-changing message of Jesus Christ, even though these areas known as the "red zones" are extremely dangerous.

Rolo's faith in Jesus Christ has been tested often. His wife abandoned him because of his dangerous Christian activity in the jungles. He went two months with very little food. The guerrillas have threatened to kill him for abandoning their cause. Yet in spite of all that he has been through, he continues to serve Jesus Christ and spread the gospel in areas hostile to Christianity. "I felt I had lost everything, but at the same time the Lord kept telling me that He was still with me," he said. "The people on the outside—pastors and Christian leaders— kept telling me that the guerrillas were just like animals and weren't worth reaching; they weren't worth giving a Bible."

Rolo, of course, disagreed and believes there is an urgency to reach the guerrillas, paramilitary, and government soldiers, as the gospel is the only hope to stop the cycle of violence. "A lot of these places are getting worse, and young people are dying sooner," he said. "There is less and less time. There is an urgency to reach these people." Rolo travels by whatever means he can, including boat, in order to reach those in the jungle by bringing them Bibles, Christian books, and solar-powered radios tuned to Christian radio stations. According to Rolo, many of these

*"Rolo" delivering Bibles to villagers*

132

people have not seen a Christian worker in more than thirty years.

Despite the great dangers that go with following Christ in this area, Rolo has seen the fruit of his labour. "It's amazing how God has multiplied the ministry in these areas where so many children have been recruited, so many people are dying or are living in despair. Countless people have been touched and are still being touched by the gospel."

This guerrilla-turned-evangelist refuses to shrink back, bravely risking possible death for advancing God's kingdom in some pretty dark places. "The rural areas and vast states here in Colombia were under the control of evil, and the people were afraid to speak up for the gospel," said Rolo. He then added, "It was when people like us went in, who weren't afraid or ashamed of the gospel, that others were led to follow us in. Many were killed and are still being killed, but whole areas have been woken up. An awakening in the Spirit is ongoing and the testimonies are flowing and the changes are even coming out on television."

Rolo said he sees some parallels in his life with the apostle Paul. "For me, this is a calling like the apostle Paul. I was willing to give my life for a wrong cause and take all those risks, being on the wrong side of things. How can I draw back now that I'm on the right side?" Even the threat of death will not stop Rolo from doing what God has called him to do.

## OUR CHALLENGE: TAKING UP THE CROSS

The stories of these committed believers ministering in Vietnam, Iraq, and Colombia—as well as scores of others who have suffered because of their passion to serve Christ—remind me of a passage in the book of Hebrews. This passage tells us that the world is not worthy of those who were persecuted for their service to God:

Others were tortured, not accepting deliverance, that they might obtain a better resurrection. Still others had trial of mockings and scourgings, yes, and of chains and imprisonment. They were stoned, they were sawn in two, were tempted, were slain with the sword. They wandered about in sheepskins and goatskins, being destitute, afflicted, tormented—of whom the world was not worthy. They wandered in deserts and mountains, in dens and caves of the earth. (Hebrews 11:35–38)

Clearly, these faithful believers are among those who "did not love their lives to the death" (Revelation 12:11). They made a decision to take up their cross knowing that it meant death—not just death to self, but physical death could also be the result. What about us? Is the world worthy or unworthy of us? What are we willing to suffer for Christ?

*Keep in mind that efforts to advance God's kingdom will always come with a reaction from the kingdom of darkness.*

Our cross to carry may not include imprisonment, beatings, or being killed for sharing the gospel like the individuals highlighted here, but we will probably face ridicule and be looked down on as narrow-minded. After all, we are constantly told by the world that there are many ways to heaven—if there is such a thing as heaven at all. In those times, we need to take courage from our persecuted brethren and not be ashamed of the gospel (Romans 1:16,17). Keep in mind that efforts to advance God's kingdom will always come with a reaction from the kingdom of darkness. If we do not spread the gospel as Jesus called us to do, we will be like some of the Christians in Vietnam who do not face persecution—because they do not evangelize.

When I hear about believers being arrested, imprisoned, raped, robbed, or killed, anger rises in me. But the reality is, this world is not going to be kind to those who have denied themselves and taken up their cross, who love and serve Jesus Christ and have given Him their lives. Satan could not defeat Jesus, so for the past two thousand years he has been targeting His followers (Revelation 12:17). The closer you are to Jesus, the closer you are to the fires of persecution!

## CONSIDER & SHARE

- When it comes to sharing the gospel, what are some ways in which you need to deny yourself?

- The concept of dying is not something we find very appealing. But according to Romans 6:5–8, what are the benefits of our dying to self? Explain whether you believe that "taking up the cross" is worth it.

- As you have read these stories from fellow believers around the world, have you decided to live your life differently? What are you going to change?

# LESSONS FROM THE PERSECUTED CHURCH

*"Learn to do good; seek justice, rebuke the oppressor;*
*defend the fatherless, plead for the widow."*
ISAIAH 1:17

I hope you have seen from these stories that our persecuted brothers and sisters in Christ around the world are just like us in so many ways. They have dreams and goals for their lives, families and friends whom they love. For the most part, they just want to live their lives in peace and serve God.

Like us, they battle against their fleshly nature. However, as you have read, their faith in Jesus has been tested beyond what most of us will likely have to experience—and they have been triumphant. So what can we learn from them?

Plenty! Not because they are super Christians, but because they were faithful to the Lord, even when they could have quit and avoided persecution. When others kept silent or denied their faith, they could not or would not. They remained devoted to Jesus. Whether they were living under an oppressive regime, or in a community that hates them, staying true to the Son of God was much more important to them than their personal comfort or possessions—or even their lives.

They understand the words of the apostle Paul when he wrote, "I have been crucified with Christ; it is no longer I who live, but Christ lives in me" (Galatians 2:20). If you are already dead, what do you have to fear? Personal safety and material things have no more hold on you.

In the West, we have mixed our desire to be Christian with our desire to have comfort and material possessions. We do not want to give up anything. I have come to envy my Christian family in places where it is hard to be a believer, not because I want to suffer or lose everything, but because I have seen what fiery trials produce—a purity of faith that far outshines any worldly goods.

My prayer is that these stories have inspired you to stand firm for Jesus. But can we do that where we live, in our materialistic society? Yes, we can.

Often I have conversations with individuals about the things of God, and usually the person I am talking with will say something like, "All religions are basically the same, and as long as you believe in something you'll be all right in the end," or, "As long as you are a good person, you'll get to heaven." At that point, I have to make a decision: do I smile and say nothing, or do I say what I know to be true and risk rejection? Jesus said He is the way, the truth, and the life, and that no one can come to the Father except through Him (John 14:6). We live in a pluralistic society where the message of the gospel and its exclusivity seems absurd, just as the message of the cross is an offence in Muslim or Communist nations. However, if many in our Christian family are willing to lay down their lives to tell others about Christ, surely I can stand up for the gospel and the One I claim to love above all others.

The reality is, we are suffering with our brothers and sisters in Christ because we are one Body, and as Paul tells us, when one part of that Body suffers, we all suffer (1 Corinthians 12:26). We are all in this together. Let us draw from each other passion, courage, faithfulness, love for our enemies, and complete devotion to Jesus! Let us fellowship in their sufferings (Philippians 3:10).

So how do we share in their sufferings and support our brothers and sisters around the world? It is quite simple: pray. When we ask them, "What do you want us to tell your Christian family in our countries?" most respond, "Pray for us!" I would encourage you to get current information about what is taking place in the Church around the world and pray, pray, and pray some more for persecuted Christians. Not only will they benefit from your prayers, but—as part of the same Body—so will you.

In my time spent with those who have suffered for their faith in Christ, I have appreciated their high regard for the Word of God. It is not that devoted Christians in the West do not believe in the authority of Scripture, but when one's physical survival depends on God providing, one is more focused on what He has to say. We in the West tend to view Scripture through the lens of a secular, prosperous culture. I have been guilty of doing that at times. We are all influenced by the materialism of a society that is not in sync with a biblical worldview.

For example, much of the preaching and teaching in North American churches is a watered-down version of the message of the cross. These life-enhancement messages and seeker-sensitive sermons would be viewed as strange and out of place in countries where believers are constantly facing danger and difficulty because of their decision to be identified with Jesus. In our desire to be acceptable to nonbelievers, we have allowed marketing techniques and worldly values to replace the unabashed call to repent and be reconciled with the holy God of the universe.

There is even a segment in the evangelical church that is actively promoting another gospel, one that says Jesus did not really die on the cross to satisfy God's wrath for our sins, because a God of love could not possibly have required that! Yes, He did—that is what the Bible clearly teaches us. (Romans 5:9 is but one of many verses on the subject.)

Our persecuted brethren do not struggle with that doctrine or with the reality of hell. In fact, it is those very teachings of Scripture that motivate them, and hopefully us as well, to preach the Good News. And it is Good News! There is a God who loves us so much that He did the unthinkable: He sent His Son to this sin-filled earth to die in our place on the cross so that all who repent and trust in Him could be made right in the sight of a holy God. Through Jesus Christ, we can be re-deemed from the hell we deserve. If you want to know what love is, just look at Jesus hanging on a tree outside of Jerusalem two thousand years ago. Most persecuted believers understand that as a given; they do not need to have material goods in this world to be assured of God's love for them. Through their faithful example, they can help us make sure that we do not forget one of the central truths of the Bible.

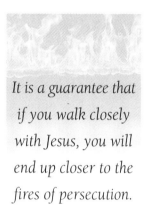

*It is a guarantee that if you walk closely with Jesus, you will end up closer to the fires of persecution.*

When the talk turns to heaven during interviews with our persecuted brothers and sisters, I often get the feeling these believers have had some kind of revelation about where their true citizenship is, and it is not wherever they live.

So many believers who have experienced incredible pain and suffering, or who live under constant threat and hardship, have a clear understanding that we are not citizens of this world, but are citizens of heaven (Philippians 3:20). One could argue that persecuted Christians are more motivated to think about heaven because their life here is so difficult and in many cases they have had so much taken from them. I would prefer to argue that we can learn from them about the importance of being focused on the things above.

As a frequent traveler, I take my Canadian passport with me everywhere I go in the world. During these international trips, I identify my nationality as Canadian. However, in reality I am a dual citizen, just like Lalani in Sri Lanka, Bukar and Hajara in Nigeria, Minh in Vietnam, and all the believers around the world. Our true citizenship is not in the country listed on our passport, the place we call home, but is in heaven.

For any disciple of Jesus, our earthly citizenship, whether living in a so-called free land or one that is hostile to Christians, is not so important. This life on earth is just temporary. The writer of Hebrews tells us, "For here we have no continuing city, but we seek the one to come" (Hebrews 13:14).

While I am proud to be a Canadian and consider this one of the best places on earth to live, as beautiful as it is, it is not forever. Only heaven is eternal. Let us make sure our desire is for our true home, the everlasting city "whose builder and maker is God" (Hebrews 11:16).

For the faithful followers of Christ, those who are engaging the enemy on the front-lines of the battle, hardship and suffering are a reality in this life. It is a guarantee that if you walk closely with Jesus, you will end up closer to the fires of persecution. That is just the way it works in the kingdom of God, as Peter informs us:

> Beloved, do not think it strange concerning the fiery trial which is to try you, as though some strange thing happened to you; but rejoice to the extent that you partake of Christ's sufferings, that when His glory is revealed, you may also be glad with exceeding joy. (1 Peter 4:12,13)

Yes, there is a cost and a danger that come with being a follower of Jesus, with having the kind of close relationship that He calls us to. But, if we keep an eternal perspective, God's Word assures us that the reward that awaits is far greater than any risk we face. Peter goes on to say, "If you are reproached for the name of Christ, blessed are you, for the Spirit of glory and of God rests upon you. On their part He is blasphemed, but on your part He is glorified" (v. 14). We are promised not only "exceeding joy" when we suffer for Christ, but we will be blessed, God's glorious Spirit will rest on us, and most importantly, God will be glorified. As followers of Christ, that is the reason we exist.

Some believers have boldly charged right into the heart of the battle; others have chosen to retreat to safety. How about you? Do you want to play it safe, or do you desire to have a deeper relationship with the Lord and a greater passion for the things of God? While there are risks to being closer to the fire, the benefits are endless and will last throughout eternity!

Will you draw closer to Jesus—and closer to the fire?

# RESOURCES

The following are a few of the resources on the persecuted Church available from The Voice of the Martyrs.

**Extreme Devotion**
*The Voice of the Martyrs*
When put to the ultimate test, they offered themselves in extreme devotion—just like the Lord they served. This daily devotional features 365 readings giving a brief account of a historical or modern-day believer who made the ultimate sacrifice for their faith. An inspirational challenge and Scripture passage accompany each selection. *(Paperback, 365 pages)*

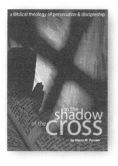

**In the Shadow of the Cross:
A Theology of Persecution and Discipleship**
*Glenn Penner*
Explore and study suffering and persecution through the entire Bible, from Genesis to Revelation. Throughout Scripture, the trials and persecutions of those who chose to live godly lives are revealed. From Abel to the prophets, from John the Baptist to the disciples, the world has always rejected (the) Truth. Included are observations and studies from nearly 200 Christian scholars, both ancient and modern. This is an excellent resource to share with a seminary student or with your pastor. *(Paperback, 315 pages)*

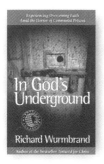

### In God's Underground
*Richard Wurmbrand*
This inspiring drama tells the story of Richard Wurmbrand's imprisonment for his faith by hardline Communists. Sentenced to "life" in a death room, he was able to rejoice in his Lord amid the most horrific conditions. It is a story of triumphant faith. *(Paperback, 276 pages)*

### The Pastor's Wife
*Sabina Wurmbrand*
Her husband had been taken, his fate unknown, and now their young son would be left alone as police arrested her. Wife of VOM founder Richard Wurmbrand, Sabina shares the heart-wrenching story of how her imprisonment in Romania speaks of the faithfulness of Christ in every situation. *(Paperback, 217 pages)*

### North Korean Voices
*The Voice of the Martyrs*
Considered the most dangerous place to be a follower of Jesus, North Korea consistently tops the world's human rights watch lists as the most repressive and closed nation on earth. Reports of inhumane actions, particularly toward Christians, continue to trickle out of the country. But there is a group of exiles who have not only escaped the "Hermit Kingdom" but also desire to go back. In *North Korean Voices*, you will meet four North Korean exiles training to take the gospel to their former homeland. *(DVD, 25 minutes)*

## Resources

The Voice of the Martyrs has many additional books, videos, and other products that will provide you with more information about the persecuted Church as well as ways to get involved in serving our suffering brothers and sisters.

In Canada, you can request a resource catalogue, order materials, or receive our free monthly newsletter by contacting our office:

The Voice of the Martyrs
P.O. Box 608
Streetsville, Ontario L5M 2C1
Website: www.vomcanada.com
Email: thevoice@vomcanada.org

If you are in the United States, Australia, New Zealand, South Africa, or the United Kingdom, contact:

**United States**
The Voice of the Martyrs
P.O. Box 443
Bartlesville, OK 74005
Website: www.persecution.com
Email: thevoice@vom-usa.org

**Australia**
The Voice of the Martyrs
P.O. Box 250
Lawson NSW 2783
Website: www.vom.com.au
Email: info@vom.com.au

**New Zealand**
Voice of the Martyrs
P.O. Box 5482
Papanui
Christchurch 8542
Website: www.persecution.co.nz
Email: thevoice@persecution.co.nz

**South Africa**
Christian Mission International (CMI)
P.O. Box 7157
1417 Primrose Hill
Email: cmi@persecution.co.za
Website: www.persecution.co.za

**United Kingdom**
Release International
P.O. Box 54
Orpington BR5 4RT
Website: www.releaseinternational.org
Email: info@releaseinternational.org

# About VOM

The Voice of the Martyrs is a non-profit charitable organization dedicated to helping, loving and encouraging persecuted Christians worldwide.

Our mission is to glorify God by serving His persecuted Church, as we seek to fulfill the words of Hebrews 13:3: "Remember the prisoners as if chained with them—those who are mistreated—since you yourselves are in the body also."

# About the Founder

 Pastor Richard Wurmbrand (1909–2001) was an evangelical minister who endured fourteen years of Communist imprisonment and torture in his homeland of Romania. Few names are better known in Romania, where he is one of the most widely recognized Christian leaders, authors, and educators.

In 1945, when the Communists seized Romania and attempted to control the churches for their purposes, Richard Wurmbrand immediately began an effective, vigorous "underground" ministry to his enslaved people as well as the invading Russian soldiers. He was arrested in 1948, along with his wife, Sabina. His wife was a slave-laborer for three years on the Danube Canal. Richard Wurmbrand spent three years in solitary confinement, seeing no one but his Communist torturers. He was then transferred to a group cell, where the torture continued for five more years.

Due to his international stature as a Christian leader, diplomats of foreign embassies asked the Communist government about his safety and were informed that he had fled Romania. Secret police, posing as released fellow-prisoners, told his wife of attending his burial in the prison cemetery. His family in

Romania and his friends abroad were told to forget him because he was dead.

After eight and a half years in prison, he was released and immediately resumed his work with the Underground Church. A couple of years later, in 1959, he was re-arrested and sentenced to twenty-five years in prison.

Pastor Wurmbrand was released in a general amnesty in 1964, and again continued his underground ministry. Realizing the great danger of a third imprisonment, Christians in Norway negotiated with the Communist authorities for his release from Romania. The Communist government had begun "selling" their political prisoners. The "going price" for a prisoner was $1,900; the price for Wurmbrand was $10,000.

In May 1966, he testified before the U.S. Senate's Internal Security Subcommittee and stripped to the waist to show the scars of eighteen deep torture wounds covering his torso. His story was carried across the world in newspapers throughout the U.S., Europe, and Asia. Wurmbrand was warned in September 1966 that the Communist regime of Romania planned to assassinate him; yet he was not silent in the face of this death threat.

Founder of the Christian mission The Voice of the Martyrs, he and his wife traveled throughout the world establishing a network of over thirty offices that provide relief to the families of imprisoned Christians in Islamic nations, Communist Vietnam, China, and other countries where Christians are persecuted for their faith. His message has been, "Hate the evil systems, but love your persecutors. Love their souls, and try to win them for Christ."

Pastor Wurmbrand authored numerous books, which have been translated into over sixty languages throughout the world. Christian leaders have called him the "Voice of the Underground Church" and "the Iron Curtain Paul."

# ABOUT THE AUTHOR

 GREG MUSSELMAN has been working with The Voice of the Martyrs (VOM) in Canada since 2000. As the Vice President of Outreach for VOM, Greg works to ensure that persecuted Christians know that they are not forgotten. Greg has reported on Christians in restricted and hostile nations in Africa, Europe, Asia, South America, and the Middle East. Along with being interviewed on numerous television and radio programs in Canada and the U.S., Greg produces video documentaries and radio and television programs for VOM. Greg is also active in sharing the message of the persecuted Church in churches, college campuses, and conferences across Canada and around the world.

A former television sports anchor and ordained minister, Greg and his wife, Arlene, live in St. Albert, Alberta, and have four children.

 TREVOR LUND has been helping people become writers and writers become authors and authors sell their books more effectively since 2005. He is a sought-after speaker on social media marketing and is a Book Shepherd at iBookShepherd.com. He is also the creator of the Make Your Book Matter Formula available at TheAuthorAcademy.com.

Trevor has seven years of experience leading people and organizations, acting as a catalyst for change and encouraging the team to change together. He has an additional seven years of experience developing and running a business enjoying challenge and variety. He has a very positive attitude and has created and promoted the annual International Life Above the Negativity Campaign since 2006.

You can find Trevor as an online pastor at RevTrev.com. On this site, through his podcast, and on Facebook, Twitter, and YouTube, Trevor helps people make their life matter. He creates resources to encourage people to live the life God intends for them. Some of Trevor's books include *Hope in Transition*, *The Freedom of Forgiveness*, *How to Know Your Hope is Secure*, *When Hope Dies*, and *The Spotted and Wrinkled Church*. You can find his ministry books at www.trevorlund.com.

# RESPONSE FORM

○ Please send me more information on how I can help the persecuted Church.

○ I already receive *The Voice of the Martyrs* newsletter. Please send a subscription to my friend at the address below. (Please include your name here: _____. We do not accept anonymous referrals.)

○ I have received Jesus Christ as my Saviour and Lord as a result of reading this book.

_____
NAME

_____
ADDRESS

_____
CITY                          STATE/PROVINCE          ZIP/POSTAL CODE

_____
PHONE                         E-MAIL ADDRESS

Please check the appropriate box(es), clip out this form, and send it to the affiliated office in your nation:

**IN CANADA:**
The Voice of the Martyrs
P.O. Box 608
Streetsville, Ontario L5M 2C1
www.vomcanada.com
email: thevoice@vomcanada.org

**IN THE UNITED STATES:**
The Voice of the Martyrs
P.O. Box 443
Bartlesville, OK 74005
www.persecution.com
email: thevoice@vom-usa.org

**IN AUSTRALIA:**
The Voice of the Martyrs
P.O. Box 250
Lawson NSW 2783
www.vom.com.au
email: info@vom.com.au
Phone: (02) 4759 3700
Fax: (02) 4759 3711

**IN NEW ZEALAND:**
Voice of the Martyrs
P.O. Box 5482
Papanui
Christchurch 8542
www.persecution.co.nz
email: thevoice@persecution.co.nz

**For a list of all affiliated offices, visit:**
www.internationalchristianassociation.org